NOTES

including
- *Life and Background*
- *Skinner and Behaviorism*
- *An Account of Utopian Literature*
- *List of Characters*
- *Critical Commentaries*
- *Utopian Communities*
- *Utopia and Communism*
- *Anti-Utopias*
- *Thoreau's* Walden *and Skinner's* Walden Two
- *Racism and Sexism in* Walden Two
- *Skinner's Language*
- *Questions for Review*
- *Selected Bibliography*

by
Cynthia C. McGowan, M.A.
University of Nebraska

and

James L. Roberts, Ph.D.
Professor of English
University of Nebraska

INCORPORATED
LINCOLN, NEBRASKA 68501

Editor

Gary Carey, M.A.
University of Colorado

Consulting Editor

James L. Roberts, Ph.D.
Department of English
University of Nebraska

ISBN 0-8220-1361-4
© Copyright 1979
by
C. K. Hillegass
All Rights Reserved
Printed in U.S.A.

Cliffs Notes, Inc.   Lincoln, Nebraska

CONTENTS

LIFE AND BACKGROUND	5
SKINNER AND BEHAVIORISM	6
THE UTOPIAN THEME	8
A BRIEF ACCOUNT OF UTOPIAN LITERATURE	9
Plato's *Republic* and Ancient Utopias	9
Sir Thomas More's *Utopia* and Skinner's *Walden Two*	11
Utopian Literature after More	17
Bellamy and Morris: Nineteenth-Century Utopias and *Walden Two*	18
LIST OF CHARACTERS	20
CRITICAL COMMENTARIES	22
Chapters 1-2	22
Chapters 3-5	23
Chapters 6-7	25
Chapter 8	26
Chapters 9-11	27
Chapters 12-13	30
Chapters 14-15	32
Chapters 16-17	34
Chapters 18-20	36
Chapters 21-22	38
Chapters 23-24	39
Chapters 25-27	40
Chapters 28-29	42
Chapters 30-32	45
Chapters 33-36	46

ESTABLISHED UTOPIAN COMMUNITIES 48

UTOPIA AND COMMUNISM 49

ANTI-UTOPIAS 50

    Samuel Butler's *Erewhon* 51

    Aldous Huxley's *Brave New World* 52

    George Orwell's *1984* 54

THOREAU'S WALDEN **AND SKINNER'S**
WALDEN TWO 55

SINS OF OMISSION: RACISM AND SEXISM
IN WALDEN TWO 57

SKINNER'S LANGUAGE 58

QUESTIONS FOR REVIEW 60

SELECTED BIBLIOGRAPHY 60

LIFE AND BACKGROUND

Burrhus Frederick Skinner (Burrhus was his mother's maiden name) was born in Susquehanna, Pennsylvania, on March 20, 1904. His parents were middle-class Protestants who offered their children (Skinner had one younger brother) vacations at summer camps, piano lessons, and other trappings of the respectable life.

In 1922, Skinner graduated from the same high school his parents had attended and decided to attend Hamilton College in Clinton, New York. Having always enjoyed school, he looked forward to an intellectual environment in which students would eagerly and voluntarily study. What he found, instead, was a campus full of students more inclined to socialize than theorize. Consequently, Skinner spent his freshman year studying languages and learning to deal with loneliness. Poetry provided him with an outlet for his feelings and having written since an early age, he turned to writing again in college, occasionally contributing poems to the campus literary magazine.

The death of his brother in 1923 contributed to the death of Skinner's idealism as he gave way to a growing skepticism within himself about the virtue and mystery of accidents in life. Never a devout believer in the religion of his family, he turned fully to intellectual observation to learn about himself and his fellow men. By his sophomore year, he was a member of several artistic circles and came to know Robert Frost, who encouraged him to write. Graduating Phi Beta Kappa in 1926, Skinner decided to try his hand at writing for one year, but was dissatisfied with the results and ended up writing a digest, commissioned by his father, on labor/management crises in the coal industry. He also read extensively during this time and found himself drawn to psychology and the theories of John B. Watson. After a brief stay in Greenwich Village and Europe, Skinner enrolled in the Harvard Graduate School where he studied psychology with a dedication unequalled by most students in any field. He studied from dawn until bedtime, allowing very little time for social activities, and he conducted experiments that ultimately led him to the discovery of "operant conditioning," which was different from earlier conditioning theories in several respects (see section on "Skinner and Behavorism").

He received his Ph.D. in 1931 and then spent five years doing research and experiments on his own, supported by research fellowships. In

1936, he accepted his first teaching job at the University of Minnesota and married Yvonne Blue, an English major at the University of Chicago.

In 1938, he published *The Behavior of Organisms: An Experimental Analysis,* which developed out of his doctoral dissertation at Harvard, a dissertation which at one time had been rejected by his committee chairman because it was "unorthodox." This publication marked the beginning of a long and successful career during which he would make his reputation as a brilliant researcher and controversial figure in twentieth-century psychology.

During the war years, Skinner was occupied with experiments teaching pigeons to guide missiles (and play ping pong), but he had started a book, *Verbal Behavior,* which was finally published in 1957. One of Skinner's other projects during the war was his invention of the "baby box." He succeeded in designing an "air crib" much like the ones for children described in *Walden Two.* His attempt to market this invention failed miserably, although his own daughter was raised in one.

In 1945, a discussion about the war and its effects prompted Skinner to write *Walden Two,* which was published in 1948. *Walden Two* received mixed reviews, and the battle between the behaviorists and the humanists began in earnest.

Since 1945, Skinner has served as Chairman of the Department of Psychology at Indiana University (he later returned to Harvard as a professor of Psychology) and has published many scholarly articles and texts, including *Science and Human Behavior* (1953), *Schedules of Reinforcement* (1957), *Contingencies of Reinforcement; A Theoretical Analysis* (1969), and his controversial *Beyond Freedom and Dignity* (1971). Since then, he has published *About Behaviorism* (1974) and his autobiography *Particulars of My Life* (Vol. 1, 1976).

B. F. Skinner's detractors and critics alike must admit that his theories have exerted a major influence on modern psychology and that "behavioral engineering" must be analyzed as a possible means of survival if we are to determine our future at all. B. F. Skinner has given us much to think about and to learn from, but the controversies surrounding his name will continue long after the man is gone.

SKINNER AND BEHAVIORISM

Behaviorists maintain that we are shaped by our environment by means of reinforcements of one kind or another. Positive reinforcement takes place when an individual is rewarded for displaying a certain kind of behavior. Negative reinforcement occurs when a behavior leads to pain or punishment. Consider the methods employed by a pet owner who is trying to housebreak a dog. When the dog has an accident, it is generally swatted with a newspaper while the owner admonishes it in an angry tone of voice. When the dog uses its paper, goes outside, or in any way carries out the owner's wishes, it is rewarded with a doggy biscuit, praise, or both. The animal learns to avoid behaviors which result in pain and to repeat behaviors which result in affection.

Behaviorism, at its most basic, is the study of the observable behaviors of humans and animals.

Behaviorists are not concerned with "mentalistic" processes, such as Freud describes in his writings, because without a knowledge and understanding of the variables influencing behavior, we can produce only speculations about the origins of a given behavior with no simple method of encouraging or eliminating a behavior. Therefore, it is likely that a behavioral psychologist would not be concerned with intangibles such as courage, free will, integrity, and the like, but would be interested in reinforcing consequences of certain behaviors that might lead an individual to repeat a behavior which others may interpret as courageous, dignified, or whatever.

The method used in training a dog, as described above, is known as conditioning. Pavlov, the Russian physiologist, is well known for his experiments in conditioning the responses of dogs. Meat was offered to the dogs, to which they responded by salivating. Then, every time the meat was offered to them, it was accompanied by the ringing of a bell. In time, the dogs associated the ringing of the bell with the meat and would salivate at the sound of the bell whether or not any meat was actually offered.

Skinner discovered a slightly different form of conditioning, "operant conditioning." Operant conditioning differs from Pavlovian conditioning in that operant conditioning defines the response in terms of its *consequences* without reference to its stimulus, which may or may not be known. Pavlovian conditioning defines the response in terms of a known, external stimulus, such as the ringing of the bell.

Skinner believes that an individual's actions are shaped and determined by the consequences they produce from the environment. Therefore, he feels that it is necessary for behaviorists to construct and control the environment in order to predict and insure that only those behaviors beneficial to society would be likely to be reinforced.

Skinner also feels that positive reinforcement works better than negative reinforcement, as it is practiced now, because negative reinforcement teaches the individual only to avoid the punishing response, which may result in the individual trying out other, equally unsatisfactory behaviors. With positive reinforcement, there is a clear correlation between a certain behavior and desirable consequences.

THE UTOPIAN THEME:
An Introduction to *Walden Two*

UTOPIA: Any condition, place, or situation of social or political perfection. Any idealistic goal or concept.

It is a fundamental disposition of humankind to concoct imaginary utopias, although the names for such places may differ. The word *utopia*, which has become the familiar designation for such states, was created by Sir Thomas More in 1516 in his book entitled *Utopia*. The term "utopia," of Greek derivation, means simply "no place." It is inevitable that people, recognizing the stupidities, corruptions, and inequities current in their society, should attempt to devise a better system for people living together.

The term "utopia" is now firmly established as an English word. It has influenced countless writers to create their own version of a utopian society. *Walden Two* represents one of the more recent additions to a long line of utopian societies.

The term "utopian" has often been extended to include various other types of works, such as the creation of imaginary gardens and earthy paradises of medieval writers which reflect the yearnings of writers dissatisfied with things as they are. In modern times Hilton's *Lost Horizon* and his Shangri-La has now passed into the vocabulary of the twentieth century as a word for the ideal haven of utopian escapism. The familiar manifestation of the utopian idea was the pastoral, idealized representation of the life of simple, happy shepherds, or else the return to various types of primitive societies, such as Rousseau's "Noble Savage," St. Pierre's *Paul and Virginia* and Chateaubriand's *Atala*. Even Shakespeare has his utopian scheme for a new and better society as outlined by Gonzalo in *The Tempest:*

> "Had I plantation of this isle, my lord,—
> . . . .
> And were the king on't, what would I do?
> . . . .
> I' the commonwealth I would by contraries

Execute all things; for no kind of traffic
Would I admit; no name of magistrate;
Letters should not be known; riches, poverty,
And use of service, none; contract, succession,
Bourn, bound of land, tilth, vineyard, none;
No use of metal, corn, or wine, or oil;
No occupation; all men idle, all;
And women too, but innocent and pure;
No sovereignty;—
....
All things in common nature should produce
Without sweat or endeavour; treason, felony,
Sword, pike, knife, gun, or need of any engine,
Would I not have; but nature should bring forth,
Of its own kind, all foison, all abundance,
To feed my innocent people.
....
I would with such perfection govern, sir,
To excel the golden age."
(The Tempest, II,i)

The history of utopian literature is extensive, even if we take the term in the strict sense of a detailed description of a nation or commonwealth ordered according to a system which the author proposes as a better way of life than any known to exist—that is, a system that could be instituted if the present one could be cancelled and people could start over. Before More's *Utopia* (1516), the number of elaborately designed utopian commonwealths is small. Most of the writings along these lines are brief, and many are misty, nostalgic backward glances at an imagined, primitive life in the "Golden Age." There is, of course, no lack of earlier literature criticizing the status quo. The great outpouring of utopian literature, however, began with Sir Thomas More's *Utopia,* and there is no reason to think that it will end with Skinner's *Walden Two.*

A BRIEF ACCOUNT OF UTOPIAN LITERATURE

PLATO'S *REPUBLIC* AND ANCIENT UTOPIAS

The earliest major work in the field was Plato's *Republic* (circa 380 B.C.), but the title "Republic" is, in fact, misleading; "state" or "civil society" would perhaps be better. The word "republic" suggests that Plato is talking about a particular form of government, a democracy, a monarchy, or a theoracy, for example. The Greek word in his title meant no more than a "state" or a "society," and Plato's ideal state is more like an enlightened monarchy than a "republic," in the modern sense of the word.

The form of Plato's work is that of a dialogue between various citizens, with one person (Socrates) largely dominating the conversation, as Frazier does in *Walden Two*. This was a feature quickly adopted by other utopian writers, and even today this format remains the most popular form for a utopian work.

The central theme of the *Republic* is the search for justice. Plato's ideal rulers would be a group of intelligent, unselfish men called the guardians or philosopher-kings, who would conduct public affairs for the good of the whole nation. The principle of communal property would be, in effect: no man calls anything his own. Gold and silver coinage would be outlawed, and there would be a rigid proscription against luxury and ostentation. Throughout the society, life would be directed by a highly moral code of conduct. An educational system for the intelligentsia would be elaborately and idealistically designed. Equality of men and women would be proposed, though with certain qualifications, and there would be a provision made in Plato's scheme for the practice of slavery, for the *Republic* establishes sharply defined class distinctions—the ruling intelligentsia; the warrior class; commoners, consisting of merchants, artisans, and laborers; and finally, at the lowest level, the slaves. In contrast, Skinner's Waldeans recognize no such gradations among their citizens, and the religious beliefs and practices in the two books are, of course, quite different. There is also a sharp difference in the treatment of families. In the *Republic,* women and children would be held in common — "there is no marrying nor giving in marriage" — and mating would be regulated to serve eugenic ends; in *Walden Two,* marriage is most important to the social structure. Ultimately, in spite of the great distance of time that separates Plato's *Republic* and Skinner's *Walden Two,* there is a great amount of similarity between them.

Other ancient utopias include Cicero's *De republica* (54-52 B.C.), especially his chapter "The Dream of Scipio," and St. Augustine's *City of God* (413-26 A.D.). While Skinner was obviously familiar with these two important works, they do not directly influence *Walden Two.*

SIR THOMAS MORE'S *UTOPIA* AND SKINNER'S *WALDEN TWO*

Sir Thomas More's *Utopia*, published in 1516, is one of the most important documents of Western civilization. It has a quality of universality, as revealed by the fact that it has fascinated readers of five centuries, has influenced countless writers, and has invited imitations by scores of "utopianists," B. F. Skinner being one of the most recent. As a result of More's book, the Greek words *ou* and *topos* (no place) became the English word "utopia" and his account of a utopia has, in one way or another, influenced all of the other imitators. Other than the specific points noted below, Skinner also adopted from More's *Utopia* the general framework and setting (More used an island called Utopia; Skinner used a community called Walden Two).

Sir Thomas More begins his *Utopia* with a discussion between More, his friend Peter Giles, and a worldwide traveler named Hythloday. There follows a lengthy day's conversation between the three men which constitutes the substance of the book. Likewise, the same basic structure is followed in *Walden Two:* three men, Professor Burris, Professor Castle, and T. E. Frazier, carry on a conversation over a period of several days and their conversation is the substance of *Walden Two*. In both cases, the conversation is dominated by one figure — Hythloday in *Utopia* and Frazier in *Walden Two*.

More's *Utopia* is divided into two parts. In Part I, we hear that Hythloday has traveled and has studied the governments of many nations and is able to discourse at length upon the relative values and shortcomings of various types of governments. His listeners advise him to publish an account of his views, but Hythloday does not believe that present governments would accept his advice nor act upon it. The majority of existing governments invariably encourage a system of flattery toward superiors and support a system of personal aggrandizement that would surely override any idealistic and philosophical proposals. (Note: flattery toward one's superiors and personal aggrandizement have also been eliminated from *Walden Two*.) Basically, in Part I of *Utopia,* Hythloday presents a critical analysis of the patterns of law, government, economics, and mores among European nations, specifically in England. His criticisms are directed particularly at the severity of the penal code, the gross inequities in the distribution of wealth, the unequal participation in productive labor, and the appropriations of farm lands for other purposes. Unlike *Walden Two,* which does not specifically attack aspects of existing governments directly, Book I of *Utopia* presents the negative aspects of governments which he suggests corrections for in Book II — that is, Book I is a statement of what is wrong with "civilization" at that time. Consequently, a discussion of the injustices, the failures, and the inadequacies of existing governments leads to a discussion of the perfection of government on a remote island called Utopia. The island of Utopia in Book II can be compared with the "ideal" or utopian society or community found at Walden Two. The following categories constitute a basic account of the patterns and concerns of life found in Utopia, concerns which are still pertinent in *Walden Two*.

Geographical Features

Hythloday, in More's *Utopia,* gives us some geographical data about the shape, length, and breadth of the island itself. He neglects, however, to mention the location on the map — that is, the latitude and the longitude are not mentioned, but he gives us enough details and physical calculations so that the reader has a sense of a real place. Burris, in *Walden Two,* lets us know that it is necessary to catch a train and then take a bus in order to reach the rural location of Walden Two, but we are never told which state it is in, or whether it is in the Midwest or in rural New England.

Country Life

In *Utopia,* a good deal of attention is paid to agriculture and country life, and it is explained that most of the inhabitants alternate between city living and country living at two-year intervals. At Walden Two, there is a strong sense of rural living, with a strong emphasis on agriculture, and there are few of the distractions of urban living.

Cities

Utopia's large island kingdom contrasts with Walden Two's community of 1,000 citizens; furthermore, the number and location of the cities in Utopia are specified and controlled, and the entire population engages in productive labor, thereby making it possible for them to operate on a *six-hour* work day. The few exemptions from farm labor or trade labor are government officials and priests. At the time of Utopia, a six-hour work day was indeed "utopian" and in Walden Two, this work day has been reduced to a *four-hour* work day, with the exemptions being rarer — that is, everyone in Walden Two must earn his/her prescribed "labor credits."

Officials

In Utopia, the leaders, or government officials (both Utopia and Walden Two have reservations about the term "leader" in the usual sense), are chosen from citizens of superior intelligence and integrity, and this body then elects a Prince to serve as its chief official. In Walden Two, the Planners and Managers, while not elected, are the ones most qualified for the position, a post by its very nature which has power, but not strong enough to be corruptive (of course, we have only Frazier's word for this).

Occupations

In Utopia, every person, with the exception of the officials and priests, practices some type of trade; therefore, because of this full participation in productive labor, the needs of the people are satisfied through a six-hour working day. In Walden Two, a lifetime commitment to a single career is not expected or even encouraged. While there are some jobs which require specific training or expertise, all members are allowed to pursue different jobs at various stages in their lives, or as their interests change. Difficult and unappealing jobs are given higher labor credits to encourage members to sign up for them; pleasant jobs, such as gardening and the like, command fewer credits, the deficit being compensated for by the nature of the work. Frazier points out that because there is no waste of manpower, and because great pains are taken by the members to increase the efficiency of tools and techniques, the working hours in a day have been reduced to four.

Community Life

In Utopia, the houses are well built and uniform but unpretentious in style. So, too, is the citizens's clothing. In both Utopia and Walden Two, no social or status distinctions can be made as a result of the type of housing or clothing of the people. In Utopia, the family is still the basic unit of society, and the oldest member is the governor of the family. Thirty different families are assigned to a large community hall and there they eat together, their food being well prepared by women best qualified for that work. This reduces the time needed for individual preparation of food and encourages good nutrition; it would be foolish to prepare an inferior dinner at home when an excellent meal is ready in the hall. In Walden Two, community dining is one of the fundamental assumptions of the organization, even though the diner can choose from one of several dining rooms; thus, the concept of communal dining is basically the same in both societies.

Economy

In Utopia, (as in almost all utopian societies) the economy is based upon communal sharing. The Utopian markets are nothing more than supply houses where *everyone* is allowed to take what he/she needs without payment. The Utopians are able to produce an abundance of food and they export the surplus to foreign countries in exchange for gold or silver for the state treasury. (In Walden Two, the surplus produce is exchanged not for gold, but for equipment or supplies which the Waldeans cannot produce; in both cases the principle is the same.) There is no private property among the Utopians, and they have no money. The wealth which they acquire by foreign trade is used only in event of war. The citizens are educated to despise jewelry and precious metals and find their use by foreigners for ostentatious decoration to be ridiculous. In Walden Two, the dress is quite functional and attractive, and there are no displays of jewelry or other ornaments. There is, furthermore, no sense of personal wealth; what the Waldeans produce becomes the property of the entire community.

Learning or Education

Education in Utopia is mainly directed toward useful learning, with the result that the citizens independently acquire the same skills and concepts as found among the ancient Greeks. They are much given to spending their leisure hours in reading. In Walden Two, the education of children is the most important enterprise of the community. Children are taught (by whom we are never told) through a system of rewards (never punishment) to enjoy those things which will make the child happy and productive, and which will in turn benefit the community. The success of Walden Two depends almost entirely on the educators of Walden Two being able to instill the principles of the community in the young and on maintaining an atmosphere which reinforces certain kinds of behaviors through a system of behavior modification. Walden Two differs from all previous utopian communities in that it is based on "behavioral engineering" which must start with the young. In this way, it eliminates (so Frazier tells us) the need for propaganda, indoctrination, and force. This kind of "useful learning" is highly valued by Waldeans. A tour of the "schoolrooms" of Walden Two shows the children getting a practical education in applied theory in all areas of endeavor.

Philosophy and Pleasure

The Utopian philosophical creed enshrines reason as the foundation for all knowledge. This leads to the belief that men's lives must be in accord with the dictates of nature; since nature prompts people to seek pleasure, pleasure is therefore regarded as the primary goal of life. Pleasure is to be restricted only if it will prove detrimental to oneself or to other people. Furthermore, careful distinctions are made concerning the values placed on the pleasures of the body and those of the mind. In Walden Two, philosophical rationalism is an assumption rather than a goal.

Marriage and Divorce

In Utopia, marriage is held in the highest regard, and any breach of chastity is severely punished. When choosing a mate, one is permitted to see the other party unclothed in order to have a better knowledge of the person whom one will wed for life. Divorce is permissible, but only under special circumstances. In Walden Two, great sanctity is placed on marriage; promiscuity is virtually non-existent. Marriage is permitted very early because of the absence of economic factors hindering such arrangements. Divorce is permitted, but it is rare; if it occurs, however, it is not considered disgraceful.

Laws and Magistrates

Utopia has no lawyers, and the magistrates or officers of the law never seek office and never wear any distinguishing attire. The state's body of laws is very brief and readily understood by all laymen. Persons who are accused of a crime plead their own cases with assistance from a judge. In Walden Two, there seems to be no need for either laws or law enforcement officers since behavior is controlled to fit the needs of the community and the factors leading to acts of violence or irresponsibility have been eliminated.

War Treaties and Alliances

In Utopia, all treaties and alliances are avoided because of a lack of trust in the fidelity of parties in such agreements. War is regarded as inhuman, something to be avoided whenever possible. Nevertheless, knowing that they must expect involvement in military conflicts at times, the government leaders of Utopia make careful preparations and have devised certain methods for conducting campaigns that have served them well. Also, their method of treating a defeated enemy with clemency is one which has proved very effective. Walden Two exists as a community and, therefore, there can be no treaties and alliances; the Planners disapprove of any kind of imperialistic policy and are actively involved in building a peaceful community.

Religion

In Utopia, there is no official religion throughout the nation. Instead, there is a considerable variety of doctrines permitted and practiced; however, atheists are not allowed to hold public office. The majority of Utopians believe in immortality and, as a consequence, they have developed a positive attitude towards death. In Utopia, those persons who have dedicated their lives to service and sacrifice correspond to the religious orders in the Christian church. Their priests are men of exceptional character and dignity. Their churches are large and beautiful, and the services interdenominational. In Walden Two, parents are free to teach their children about religion, but there is no formal religious education. There are Sunday services, but these seem to appeal to the aesthetic sense, instead of being lectures in theology. There is an implicit feeling in Walden Two that formal religion is not essential in a community predicated on mutual respect, caring, and behavioral science. While Frazier utilizes *some* of the principles laid down by Jesus Christ, he finds most religious tenets governing behavior to be based on a system of guilt and punishment, a system which he believes to be inefficient for insuring "good behavior."

In general, both societies advocate justice for all citizens, communal ownership of property, and a happy, productive community. Both attempt to remove the causes of dissension and insure that the behavior of individuals will benefit the larger society, but both approach these problems from vastly different perspectives and with antithetical solutions.

UTOPIAN LITERATURE AFTER MORE

During the century following More's *Utopia*, the utopian vogue flourished, set off by the interest which More's book generated and given added impetus through the discoveries of new lands and the fascinating primitive and exotic races encountered in those regions. Thus, many books which are often attributed to the genre of utopian literature are more accurately classified as travel books or fantasies. Remember, Columbus's discovery of America occurred only twenty-four years prior to the publication of More's *Utopia*.

Sixteen years after More's *Utopia*, its impact is seen in Rabelais's first book of *Pantagruel* (1532) in which a section is entitled "The Expedition to Utopia." Actually the narrative in no way resembles Utopia, but there are incidental parallels. Details of the voyage from France to Utopia are in a general way reminiscent of More's account of the travels of Hythloday. And it is noteworthy that Rabelais called the inhabitants of Utopia the Amaurotes, a word derived from More's name for the capital city of Utopia.

Subsequently, More's influence is seen in Montaigne's famous essay "Of Cannibals," which gives an account of a primitive tribe of South American Indians; while treating their life-style in toto, he pays special attention to their choice of leaders, mode of warfare, and their treatment of captives. This work was a notable contribution to the vogue of fictionalized travel literature, which includes, in addition to More's *Utopia*, such works as Defoe's *Robinson Crusoe*, Swift's *Gulliver's Travels*, Voltaire's *Candide* (the visit to El Dorado), and a host of later major and minor documents. Sir Francis Bacon's *New Atlantis* (the title is taken from the mythical kingdom of Atlantis in Plato's *Republic,*) written around 1622, combines travel and adventure with the utopian theme. It purports to relate the discovery by an exploring expedition in the Pacific Ocean of an island where the natives have developed a society offering much to admire. The goal of the common good is sought after thorough learning and justice. The principal attention of the account is focused on an elaborate academy of science. Bacon's idea that the advancement of human welfare can best be achieved through the systematic exploration of natures is akin to Frazier's theory in *Walden Two* that a study of the behavioral processes will lead to a more perfect society.

BELLAMY and MORRIS: NINETEENTH-CENTURY UTOPIAS AND *WALDEN TWO*

Bellamy's *Looking Backward* (1888) and William Morris's *News from Nowhere* (1890-91) are often discussed by the group at Walden Two and sometimes are compared to various aspects of the Walden Two experiment. The former is the most successful and best known of American utopias, and it presents a vision of a glorious future society. It is set in Skinner's own Boston. Julian West, a young aristocratic Bostonian falls asleep in a hypnotic trance in 1887, and through a remarkable set of circumstances, is awakened in the year 2000. His host family in this new age introduces him to their amazing society, explaining their institutions and the rationale for their system.

The new Boston of 2000, Julian West discovers, is a city of beauty and grace, with many splendid public buildings, reflecting an undreamed of prosperity; but, more important, it is populated by people who are remarkably healthy and happy. The basic reason for these conditions is that equality has been attained throughout the population. There are no more rich, no more poor.

The first lesson West learns is that all industry and all institutions are under the control of the national government, a system which he is informed has proven to be far more effective than the earlier one of free, private enterprise because of the elimination of wasteful competition. These enormous nationwide political and industrial institutions are structured on the plan of a military organization. Money has been outlawed, but a substitute means of transacting personal business has been devised. Every individual is given a monthly allowance in the form of a credit card, a kind of punch card to record his expenditures. This method permits individuals to exercise judgment and taste in the way they like to live. Some will set a better table than others, some acquire larger houses, and some will travel extensively, but everyone's allowance is the same.

The extraordinary efficiency of the entire business structure is explained partly by superior management, as has been said, but also partly because they have eliminated several costly and time-consuming activities, thereby freeing the citizens for more productive work. There is no Army, no Navy, or police force; likewise, there are no lawyers, bankers, or salesmen.

Education is regarded as important and is continued until citizens reach twenty-one years of age. At twenty-one, everyone enters the work force, "the industrial arm," where he/she will serve until the age of forty-five. Women and men are treated equally with respect to education, career in the work force, and compensation. There is some distinction made regarding the occupations of men and women, and there are provisions for pregnancy.

Bellamy's optimism for the future of mankind is seen in his prediction that there will be piped-in home entertainment, obtained by merely pressing buttons or turning knobs for sermons, lectures, or a wide selection of musical programs. He does not develop this aspect of modern living at length, however, for his chief interest lies in the fields of economics and sociology.

In William Morris's *News from Nowhere,* the author offers his vision of a bright future for England. The narrator of the novel goes to bed in his home in a London suburb one night in 1890, but when he wakes he finds himself in strange surroundings. The people he meets talk about events that occurred in the year 2001 as though they were past history.

Radical changes have transformed England both in appearance and in its social patterns. The new society is structured according to the pattern of ideal communism: there is no money nor is there private property; there is perfect equality for every citizen. Labor is shared by every member of the community. These are all familiar attributes of utopian societies. One of the distinctive features of Morris's plan is that labor is regarded as a pleasure rather than as a necessary chore, the reason being that all the people work at the tasks that each is best at; consequently, they take pride in the product of their labors.

Morris's utopia is the natural outgrowth of his lifelong devotion to two causes: first, his conviction that the workman of Medieval times was a happy man and a fulfilled artist, and second, his political involvement in the Socialist movement.

Morris, like Bellamy, predicts a brighter future for mankind, with men and women equal, healthy, and happy; but he differs radically in his belief that we must not discard "modernity" with its advancing technology and complex organization. In fact, Morris was provoked into writing *News from Nowhere* as a refutation of *Looking Backward.*

Beginning with H. G. Wells, there is a body of work which could be characterized as part utopian and part science fiction. Most of these works, like Wells's *The Time Machine* and *The War of the Worlds,* are primarily science fiction. Of Wells's work, the closest to a classical utopian piece is *A Modern Utopia.* It is utopian specifically in that Wells held a firm belief in the progress of mankind toward perfection; hence, he confidently pictured a bright future. The term "modern" in the title was meant to convey the idea that he intended to keep his society within the realm of reasonable possibility, avoiding any excessively visionary treatment of the theme. For that reason, he was unwilling to adopt certain features that were traditional among the majority of earlier utopianists.

In conclusion, the selected utopian societies described, without exception, developed systems which strived for equality and justice. Equality is attempted in nearly every instance through communal sharing of property and the elimination of money, through equitable sharing of labor, community rearing of children, and often community dining. Plain, uniform clothing is usually prescribed, and any kind of luxury or ostentation is discouraged. The governments are made up of carefully selected elders of demonstrated character and competence. Variations appear regarding the question of communal sharing of women, proposed by Plato but rejected by More. The acceptance of slavery in the community, approved by both Plato and More, is not adopted by their followers. Clearly, Skinner's *Walden Two* is another in a long line of established utopian works and, as such, it offers us one more variation on a theme.

LIST OF CHARACTERS

Professor Burris

A university professor who was in graduate school with T. E. Frazier. Throughout the novel, he exercises caution and common sense and represents a middle point between Frazier's "radical" position and Castle's "reactionary" one.

Rogers

Burris's ex-student who had read Frazier's account of Walden Two and comes to discuss utopian societies with Burris.

Steve Jamnik

Rogers's friend who is also interested in utopian societies. Steve and his girlfriend will ultimately join the Walden Two community.

Barbara Macklin

Rogers's girlfriend who accompanies the group to Walden Two; she is uncomfortable there. Her skepticism about Walden Two creates a struggle for Rogers, who is attracted to both Barbara and to the ideas of Walden Two. Barbara is described as being beautiful and sophisticated.

Mary Grove

Steve Jamnik's girlfriend who decides with Steve to become a part of Walden Two. She is depicted as being of average looks and intelligence.

T. E. Frazier

The moving force behind the establishment of Walden Two; the central character of the book.

Augustine Castle

A professor of Philosophy who accompanies the group to Walden Two for the intellectual adventure; he functions as the antithesis of Frazier.

Mrs. Rachel Meyerson

The woman in charge of "Clothing for Women" at Walden Two.

Mr. Meyerson

The medical examiner who shows the group through the medical facilities.

Miss Ely

The dentist of Walden Two.

Mrs. Nash

One of the people who work with the children.

Simmons

Along with Frazier, he was one of the people instrumental in establishing Walden Two.

CRITICAL COMMENTARIES

Chapters 1-2

Walden Two begins with two young men who have been recently discharged from military service and who have come to talk with Professor Burris in his university office. The two young men have been overseas together, have gone through the war, and are now seeking to found some type of idealistic society. One of the young men, Rogers, has developed a keen social conscience and feels powerless to change existing social evils in present-day society. He is dissatisfied with the options open to him, and he remembers a discussion of utopian societies in Professor Burris's class some years ago. A friend of his, Steve Jamnik, proved sympathetic to Rogers's ideas, and the two of them have come to discuss their interest in investigating the possibility of working towards a more perfect system. Talking with Professor Burris, the young men discover that Burris's ideas about a utopian community came from T. E. Frazier, the same man who wrote an article about utopias that Steve and Rogers had read. They decide to write to Frazier and inquire about Walden Two, the name of his community.

Frazier responds with an invitation for them to visit Walden Two. A group consisting of Burris, his colleague Professor Augustine Castle of the Philosophy Department, Rogers and Steve Jamnik, along with their respective girl friends, Barbara and Mary, accept the invitation to visit the community. To get to Walden Two, they first catch a train and later transfer to a bus which takes them to the rural setting of Walden Two, where they are met by T. E. Frazier.

Although we have been informally introduced to Frazier in the initial chapter (Burris remembers him as a "queer duck" back in graduate school), our formal introduction begins when he meets the bus; he is described as a rather ordinary person who anticipates the needs of his guests with an assurance that irritates Burris.

The work, *Walden Two,* begins as do so many utopian novels, with a *select* group of people expressing their dissatisfaction with an existing society and with a desire to explore alternative life-styles. It is significant that *Walden Two* is set immediately after World War II, a war that changed our way of thinking in so many ways. It is also important to note that since this book deals with the psychology of society and human relationships, that psychology as an applicable science received a tremendous boost during and after World War II, when psychological tests were administered on a large-scale basis to service men to determine, among other things, aptitude and stability under stress.

Later on, even though we are to learn a great deal about the physical layout of Walden Two, we are never able to pinpoint it geographically, except to say that it is near a town called Canton, located in a rural area. With few exceptions, nearly all utopias avoid specific placement, thus giving the impression that they could exist anywhere.

Chapters 3-5

In these chapters, we are taken on a tour of the physical layout of the community, with Frazier as our guide. The character's impressions (and by extension, our impressions) of Walden Two are always supplemented with explanations from Frazier of the utilitarian aspects of life in the community and with lectures on the principles which govern even the most commonplace practices.

The discussion of the sheep and the lawn leads to an allegorical projection of the problem of maintaining a social order in which there are skeptics who challenge the basic assumptions of the existing society in the quest for individual freedom. The sheep here are symbolic representations of humankind, and the sheepdog Bishop symbolizes the threat of force which polices the flock and maintains the status quo. As we will see later, Frazier will liken himself to a god who sets a system in motion and then retires to watch it operate in the same conceptual manner as did the god of the seventeenth- and eighteenth-century British deists. In this case, we can see that while God, or Frazier, may set up a code of ethics to live by, certain religious or political leaders (or even sheepdogs) enforce the code, while the majority follow or conform sheeplike, out of respect for tradition or fear of physical reprisal.

In Chapter 3 and elsewhere, we find that Walden Two is fashioned with an awareness of how other utopias (such as Edward Bellamy's and H. G. Wells's) have either theoretically failed or succeeded.

The interaction of the characters is a kind of "behavioral engineering" on the part of B. F. Skinner. The characters as such are never realized as fully developed human beings, as one would expect to find in a novel; instead, they represent different points of view in an argument. If we see Walden Two itself as the premise of a formal argument, then Frazier is its staunch protagonist, Castle is its antagonist, and Burris is a kind of synthesis between the two points of view. The effect of this on the reader is to mistrust Frazier's blind support while becoming annoyed at Castle's bad manners and his trivial nit-picking, especially his specious arguments. This results in a subtle manipulation of the reader by Skinner so that the only ultimate possible identification is with Burris, who, though aware of the limitations of Walden Two, feels that these limitations are far outweighed by their advantages and, therefore, chooses Walden Two for himself. Thus, by anticipating all of the possible arguments against Walden Two, Skinner controls the reader's reaction so skillfully that the reader accepts Walden Two as the utopian ideal through Burris's reasoning.

Throughout the book, Burris will maintain a middle-of-the-road position, and Castle will become increasingly more antagonistic toward the community and toward Frazier (until ultimately, his intolerance becomes unbearable to Burris). As a result of Castle's behavior, Frazier and Walden Two are seen in a better light.

In Chapter 4, Burris strays from the group (led by Frazier) and finds himself in the middle of a party of Walden Two residents who draw him in with friendly, clever remarks. Although he acknowledges them to be charming and sociable, he feels strangely paralyzed and speechless. He determines that because he does not understand their life-styles and habits, he feels like an alien. Uncomfortable, he makes an inane comment and rushes off to find his group.

Frazier introduces Burris to Mrs. Meyerson, the woman in charge of Clothing for Women and after a brief exchange, she leaves with Barbara and Mary. Frazier then begins to speak about the achievements of Walden Two; in particular, he cites the tea service they are about to use. The antagonism between Castle and Frazier continues as Castle trivializes the triumphs of "domestic engineering." Frazier promises "heavier fare" later and squelches Castle by showing him how much is gained in efficiency and time by even the smallest labor-saving innovations.

Chapter 5 opens with a discussion of the women of Walden Two. Frazier assures Burris that representative sampling was attempted and that the general attractiveness of the women is not a result of selectivity, but a result of the women's avoiding the latest styles and faddish hairdos. Mrs. Meyerson explains that by encouraging "tasteful dress" and by playing up one's individual attractiveness, every woman can be striking and cosmopolitan. Frazier adds also that avoiding fads and "in" styles reduces consumerism and competitiveness. The discussion is then directed to the children who walk by on their way to the evening meal. Frazier explains that young children take their meals together until their seventh birthday, at which time they are allowed to eat with the adults in the main dining room.

Burris returns to their previous discussion of attire and comments that men in Walden Two tend to dress more informally than women. Frazier argues this is not a sex difference (although his stating it doesn't make it so). He explains that nothing in the community calls for either dressing up as a sign of status or dressing down as a sign of protest; what they strive for is a neat informality that corresponds to the basic life-style of Walden Two.

The chapter ends with the group watching a birthday party and with Burris noticing that Frazier showed "an exaggerated expression of affection" for the children. Although Frazier is generally characterized as being primarily interested in the scientific aspects of the community, he will be shown occasionally, as here, responding to the people themselves.

Chapters 6-7

Chapter 6 is focused on there being no large crowds or group assemblies and on the entertainment offered in Walden Two. Burris is surprised at the number of small, quiet groups in the common rooms and admits that he expected crowds of noisy people. Frazier explains that crowds are neither useful nor interesting and are not profitable unless one is suffering from loneliness. As an example, he cites the situation of an average housewife who enjoys crowds because she has lacked company during the day. Frazier explains that loneliness is not a problem in Walden Two and that people gather in small groups to explore their common interests. He says further that the people of Walden Two have many choices of entertainment—the theater, movies, concerts, and discussion groups on timely topics. It is intimated here and will be discussed more fully later, that there is an absence of competitive sports in Walden Two. We learn later that competition of any kind is frowned upon because, as Frazier says in this chapter, "We are not hero worshippers."

Castle asks about lectures and lecturers, and Frazier replies that lecturing is an inefficient, obsolete method of disseminating culture. Frazier maintains that those interested in a specified topic could just as well read about it themselves as listen to someone else, and that there is a difference between lecturing and entertainment and that some members of Walden Two, if they are going to spend time listening to someone, would prefer to be entertained than lectured to. Castle then asks if a large group wouldn't be interested in a discussion of a political nature; Frazier laughs and says that very few people in the community would be interested in politics because everything they do within the community *is* political. Later, we find out that the basic reason for a lack of interest in politics is that there is a Walden Two political ticket which looks after the interests of Walden Two, and that everyone votes a straight Walden Two ticket.

Castle, always looking for a weak point in Frazier's argument, asks if there isn't an unmanageable crowd in the dining room at meal times. Frazier explains that daily schedules are staggered, an arrangement which results in a need for less equipment, fewer utensils, smaller rooms and no crowding. Frazier goes on to say that not everyone is required to eat at a certain time with everyone else, thereby enjoying a schedule which offers a flexibility and a diversity that is psychologically healthful.

Notice that Frazier is characterized in the last paragraph as a "shepherd" moving "his flock to another point of interest." This contributes to the underlying religious motif of this book and prepares us for the later parallel between Frazier and God.

Chapter 7 provides us with a description of the dining rooms and the reason for their being decorated in the styles of different periods and/or cultures. The food is served cafeteria or buffet style and provides Frazier with the opportunity to compare commercial bakers and cooks with those of Walden Two. He also gives another example of "domestic engineering" — the tray which has been modified so that it is efficient to wash from a labor-saving point of view. This domestic engineering shows a lack of cognizance of the importance of ecology-saving measures and techniques since detergents are used indiscriminately. The contemporary reader may object to some of Walden Two's techniques on the grounds that they contribute to pollution and waste, but this was not a problem recognized by citizens at large at the time Skinner wrote the book.

Chapter 8

This chapter begins with a description of the economy of Walden Two. There is no currency as we know it; instead, there is a system of "labor credits," and members work only *four* hours a day, one of the acknowledged achievements of Walden Two. By assigning different credits to various jobs, Walden Two has avoided adopting the class structure inherent in the system of *Brave New World,* to which Castle refers. The basis for the labor credit system was adopted and modified from the utopia of Edward Bellamy's *Looking Backward*. The mention of these other utopias suggests that Walden Two is constructed so that the pitfalls of other utopias will be avoided while the successes of the others will be emulated.

Frazier goes on to explain the duties and the responsibilities of the Planners and the Managers, but he explains that no job carries any more prestige or status than any other. Also, all honorific titles are avoided. The Planners oversee the entire management of Walden Two, and they are assisted by the Managers, who are in charge of the services of Walden Two.

To respond to Castle's skepticism of the ability of a community to function on a four-hour work day, Frazier explains how their four-hour day is as productive as an eight-hour day in the world at large. First, one hour is reduced because the workers are able to work more skillfully than others and because four hours of working is equivalent to five hours otherwise. Second, because no one works for a profit hungry boss, but works for themselves, "waste is avoided, workmanship is better, deliberate slow downs unheard of." Third, those people working eight-hour days work in part for those who do not work — the leisure class, the sick, the disabled, and the criminals. In Walden Two, everyone works, even the children, though at jobs consistent with their youth and inexperience. Fourth, Walden Two makes the best possible use of labor-saving devices and mechanization, which Frazier asserts are not used consistently or to the best advantage in the rest of the world. Further, many jobs have been eliminated entirely and even necessary jobs have been streamlined. Finally, Frazier states that the women are free to work because the community has industrialized housewifery. All of the characters seem impressed with this explanation and the achievement.

We learn that while the standard of living is consistently high in Walden Two that unnecessary consumption is not encouraged. Consequently, there is never a threat of a shortage of necessities. The end of Chapter 8 corresponds to the end of the group's first full day at Walden Two.

Chapters 9-11

Burris gets up early the next morning, sees Mary up also, and the two knock gently at Steve and Rogers's door. There is no answer and, assuming that the two young men are still asleep, Burris and Mary go off to breakfast. During breakfast, Burris is delighted to discover that the previously strained relationship between them no longer exists, and they enjoy conversing with each other on an informal basis. They are soon joined by Steve and Rogers, who have been out walking, and they all gather to find out what their work assignment is. The woman in charge offers them "window-washing," which they accept with equanimity.

They organize themselves into pairs in order to make the job go more quickly. Burris notes that Steve and Rogers work smoothly together. Castle works earnestly but awkwardly, and Mary is efficient, but Barbara does not seem to be at home with the task and makes wisecracks to cover her embarrassment. By noon they have finished the task, and Burris decides that it is better than grading student papers, but Castle feels better equipped to grade student papers. Already this early in the work, Skinner is letting us know that Castle and Barbara will be the two people who will not be sympathetic to the Walden Two experiment and will not fit into the ideal society that is found there.

In Chapter 10, Frazier explains that the secret of the economic success of Walden Two is that the community has avoided returning to "the goat and loom," which means that they have not made the mistake of some utopian societies of trying to return to primitive methods of agriculture by rejecting or ignoring modern technological advances. Again, Walden Two is based upon a system which has taken into account the faults found in the works of Rousseau or Fournier, in which man rejected everything in modern society and tried to return completely to a primitive society. As Frazier points out, "our point of view here isn't atavistic. . . . We look ahead, not backwards."

Walden Two is still based partly upon farming and industry. The major difference between Walden Two and other communities is that at Walden Two hard work has not been done away with; instead, they have done away with work that is "uncreative and uninteresting."

Frazier leads them quickly to a sort of giant food locker where the community produce is kept. Because jobs are flexible, it is possible to amass a large number of people to prepare foods for storage at harvest time and still not be faced with the problems of other cultures which employ large numbers of migrant workers at harvest time and then have no place for the migrant workers to go after the harvest is over. The labor credit system at Walden Two prevents this sort of thing from occurring.

The dairy is the next stop in their guided tour of Walden Two. As the group talks to the manager in charge of dairy products, they realize that he has no real awareness of the principles of behavorial engineering, but instead is concerned with the welfare of the cows, the amount of butter fat produced annually, and the practical aspects of dairy farming. Burris, at this point, realizes that Frazier has very little practical knowledge. While he understands the principles behind each job, he could "not make a corn soufflé or clear a pond." Burris feels that Frazier may be missing something — the quiet pride and assurance that comes with self-sufficiency.

Presently, Mrs. Meyerson joins the group. She is late because the rehearsal for Bach's *B Minor Mass* went badly. They visit several other buildings, a woolen shop, a wood-working shop and a machine shop, but the shops are largely deserted. This surprises Frazier who explains uneasily that people are probably working outdoors because of the nice weather. They go on to a clothing shop where Mary demonstrates the embroidery stitch that her grandmother taught her. Her contribution is appreciated, but no one thanks her as they leave. This is because the Walden Two code does not encourage gratitude to an individual but encourages gratitude to the entire community and a renewed commitment to making the community work. Mary is pleased and does not seem to miss the individual expression of thanks. Since it is nearly five o'clock, they decide to wait for a truck to take them back to the main building. As they stretch out on a grassy bank beside the road, Frazier begins to ask Rachel Meyerson about the Bach concert. She and Frazier agree that the group should attend the late supper and then go to the theater. Frazier asks Rachel to join them, but she has other plans. The truck arrives and drops them off at their quarters, and all go indoors except Burris and Mrs. Meyerson. He asks her about the Bach chorale. Burris is pleased and looks forward to the concert with anticipation. Nearby, Frazier asks Castle what he thinks of the "Lovely Lady," meaning the community of Walden Two. Mrs. Meyerson turns away from Burris to listen to Frazier and Castle's discussion. Since she has not understood the metaphor, she might in fact think that they are referring to her. As Frazier extends the metaphor, Mrs. Meyerson interrupts confusedly to ask what they are saying. Frazier's answer is abstruse and Mrs. Meyerson dismisses him with a laugh. Frazier and Mrs. Meyerson walk off together talking and laughing. Burris tells Castle that the lovely lady's name is Rachel. Here he is of course referring to Mrs. Meyerson and not to the community.

In Chapter 11, Burris notes the many alternatives open to them in terms of entertainment. As the group assembles for supper, they plan to attend the eight o'clock Bach chorale. Although each event is described on a notice on the bulletin board, there is no attempt to advertise. Frazier tells them that the bulletin board elicits excitement from the members, unaccustomed as they are to neon signs and garish lights. The events are shorter than those we are accustomed to, but Frazier explains that they are the right length to hold one's attention and that the time spent allowing for bad weather and transportation are eliminated in Walden Two so that it is not necessary to extend a concert for two or three hours to make it worth one's while.

Steve and Mary decide to go to a young people's dance with several young people that they have met. The others eat in the Swedish room and discuss leisure time. Castle suggests that it may be boredom that motivates the members to plan so many activities. Frazier suggests that it is due to enthusiastic patronage of the arts and asserts that the right conditions exist in Walden Two to produce not only science and technology but art as well. Burris draws him into a discussion of what those conditions are, and Frazier describes the obstacles that hinder creativity in the outside world.

At one point Burris suggests that heredity may be important, but Frazier exclaims that it is the environment which is of prime importance. Since B. F. Skinner is a behavioral psychologist, it stands to reason that the psychological environment of Walden Two would be all-important and have the utmost significance to him in producing the Golden Age which Frazier anticipates in the book.

Already late, the group hurries on to the Bach chorale. Burris finds himself unable to concentrate on the music, besieged as he is by random thoughts of the supper conversation. It is as if a violent struggle is taking place within him, at times accepting and at times refuting Frazier's assertions. At the end of the chorale, Burris realizes that everyone is applauding enthusiastically, but he remembers little of it because it came almost as a physical assault to be blocked out.

Although we will go on in the next few chapters to discuss more of the practical aspects of Walden Two, we can assume that each character is trying to evaluate for himself or herself the relative advantages of Walden Two as compared to the advantages of their own lives. Although Castle and Barbara seem to have the least effort rejecting the way of Walden Two as a valid life-style, the others will struggle much harder to come to terms with this new, experimental utopian society.

Chapters 12-13.

The next morning the group visits the schools. Many of the children are outdoors practicing Euclidian geometry and experimenting with surveying equipment. Frazier presses them onto the nursery where they are met by Mrs. Nash. As Mrs. Nash shows them around, they see babies of all ages in individual cubicles. Controls on the cubicles allow those in charge to filter the air and to adjust the temperature. This frees the babies from having to wear restraining clothes (thus saving on laundry) and keeps the babies's environment germ-free. The people in charge (both men and women work in the nursery) observe the babies closely so as to maintain sanitary conditions within the cubicles.

This innovation of the "baby box" is not a fanciful device created for this novel, but, in fact, was a real invention of B. F. Skinner. He designed a rather large piece of furniture with a big glass window, the purpose of which was to allow a baby to mature in a sanitary, germ-free, temperature-controlled environment while freeing the mother for other tasks. Skinner raised one of his daughters in one such apparatus and attempted to market the cubicles on a large scale. The devices were tentatively named "Heir Conditioners." Because most Americans could not accept this scientific approach to parenting, the endeavor was a commercial flop.

Castle asks about the possible effects of what he sees to be the absence of "mother love." This is met with laughter, and Frazier explains that the children receive affection not only from their biological parents but also from the entire community. In fact, what is absent is the irritation and annoyance of parents who are overworked and unable to meet the emotional demands of their children. The group then moves on to a slightly older group of children.

In the quarters for the children who are one to three years of age, the children sleep unclothed, except for diapers. The temperature and humidity are controlled on the same principle as that for small babies. Here the children are at play, and soon some women arrive to take them on a picnic. Not all of the children go, and Castle asks how they cope with jealousy and envy. Mrs. Nash is puzzled and doesn't understand Castle's question. Frazier explains that Mrs. Nash came to the community when she was twelve and that jealousy is not one of her present emotions, which accounts for her puzzlement at Castle's question. Frazier explains that some of the negative emotions have been eliminated by means of a series of psychological challenges designed to teach the child to deal more beneficially with frustrations and jealousy. Frazier says that these and other negative emotions are fostered by a competitive society and simply serve no purpose in Walden Two. He goes on to say that destructive emotions can be eliminated when the child realizes that problems cannot be solved by aggression but must be reasoned out. He promises to explain the principles of behavioral engineering shortly.

Chapters 14-15

In Chapter 14, Frazier asserts that "each of us has interests which conflict with the interest of everyone else." Society always wins in the long run and enslaves the individual. In the outside world, the individual is coerced into behavior that benefits society by the threat of outside force; in Walden Two, on the other hand, the aim is to work out a method of experimental modification that will result in the individual behaving in a certain way not out of fear or because of force, but because it serves the interest of the individual. One of the early planners, Simmons, and Frazier began by looking over some of the great works of the world to discover how man developed a moral or ethical code of behavior. In the course of their research, they examined "Plato, Aristotle, Confucius, the New Testament, Puritan divines, Machiavelli, Chesterfield, [and] Freud" to find useful principles of behavioral control. The solution they chose was similar to the advice ("love thine enemies") of Jesus, though Frazier points out that Jesus has been regrettably misinterpreted through the ages. It is useless to rage against circumstance and to expend energy in hatred; what Jesus taught was the technique for channeling those emotions into positive and profitable endeavors.

These principles have manifested themselves in the present-day method of treatment known as rational-emotive therapy. The premise of this theory is that the individual alone is responsible for and in control of his/her feelings; by struggling with old habits, we can learn to redirect negative emotions into, at worst, indifference — allowing a peace of mind that would be impossible to achieve in any other way.

Frazier relates some practical applications for this theory. For example, he explains that children are taught to be patient and to bear frustrations by a deliberate withholding of lollipops, and then later, by being given lollipops which they are asked not to lick for several hours. Frazier insists that this teaches them self-control. Similarly, they are taught to deal with envy during mealtimes, when some children are allowed to eat before others. Castle sees this as psychological torture, but Frazier insists that this is a means of freeing the children from being enslaved and tortured by emotions that they have never learned to control.

Castle continues to defend traditional practices in the world at large on the basis that some people triumph no matter what the conditions of their lives. Frazier counters that there is no virtue in accident and that the practices of Walden Two may well enable more than just a few to triumph and lead creative and fulfilling lives.

In Chapter 15, we have an example of "behavioral engineering" in the schedules of the "slightly older children." The first year of life is spent in the cubicle, and the second and third years are spent in a small room with a controlled environment. The three- and four-year-olds sleep on cots in a dormitory and begin wearing regular clothes. The five- and six-year-olds sleep in small groups, and seven-year-olds share small rooms until they turn thirteen, at which time they are moved to an adult building where two share a room until a need for greater privacy or marriage motivates the individual to build larger quarters or refurnish the old room. In this way control by authority is relaxed as the child begins to take control of him/herself. Similarly, in the dining room, the small children eat in separate quarters; then at thirteen, the choice is left entirely up to the young adult.

As the group tours the "workshops, laboratories, studies and reading rooms used in lieu of classrooms," they grow more and more puzzled. Instead of being confined to one room where they absorb information, the children apply the things that they learn or else they intuit things for themselves in such a nontraditional manner that it is difficult for the newcomer to see that actual learning is taking place.

Burris wishes to ask Frazier about the children's good behavior, but realizes that this is an offshoot of the happy, productive non-restrictive atmosphere of Walden Two. Later, Frazier takes the group outside and begins to talk about the teacher's role in Walden Two. In the outside world, there is such a division between home life and school, that the teacher spends a great deal of time re-educating students and changing certain habits which the child learned at home. This division is absent in Walden Two, and the extra time can be spent much more productively. Frazier explains that standardization is unnecessary and unhealthy, and that at Walden Two, children's talents and abilities are allowed to develop at individual rates.

Because no economic or prestigious value is attached to education at Walden Two, learning is its own reward and children teach themselves and respond to challenges. Burris asks about those who might want to go on to higher education, and Frazier explains that those who want to go on and study in a university are given preparations for the entrance examinations and are then admitted to graduate schools.

Burris is skeptical about the quality of the libraries and laboratories that Walden Two can provide, but again Frazier shows that even a small library kept up to date by efficient help can be better utilized than a huge library full of unused pamphlets and outdated materials which are useful to no one. He continues, saying that anatomy is taught in the slaughterhouse, "botany in the fields, genetics in the dairy and poultry house, chemistry in the medical building and in the kitchen and dairy laboratory."

Castle defends traditional education although he admits that it is difficult to argue against an accomplished fact, such as the success of education in Walden Two. But he is dubious about the motivation of the student. When pressed, Castle admits that the "standard motive" of the traditional student is a fear of low grades, the prestige of a degree, and a greater salary given to those who are more educated. Frazier dismisses these as unworthy of the truly curious student; he prefers the motivation that babies demonstrate, which is the natural curiosity and desire to manipulate the world around them, a desire which is usually thwarted by parents, the educational system, and the culture at large. By encouraging natural curiosity in Walden Two, it is possible to produce an alert and inquiring adult. Burris mentions the "neurotic geniuses" familiar in outside society, but Frazier questions the culture's diagnoses of neurosis and the virtue to be found in a culture which by accident produces a few brilliant, unhappy individuals.

As the discussion goes on, Frazier reveals, much to the surprise of Burris and Castle, that the controlled conditions of environment for children in Walden Two has not led to a standardization of I.Q. and talent, but that, in fact, a wide diversity exists in the I.Q.s, talents, and physical abilities of the members. The chapter ends with Castle stubbornly maintaining that is is impossible to realize spontaneity and freedom through a system of complete control.

Chapters 16-17

Chapter 16 takes up the question of teenage marriage, birth, and child care. One of the easiest ways to shock the conservative individual anxious to preserve the status quo is to challenge the family unit as we have known it in modern times and to acknowledge the validity of teenagers's emotions and sexuality. Frazier explains that there is no reason to delay marriage or childbearing in a system which encourages self-sufficiency and a mature, responsible attitude toward life. He says that most couples marry in their middle to late teens and that the average mother is eighteen at the birth of her first child. Frazier anticipates the common arguments that early marriage is a characteristic of primitive and backward cultures. He immediately counters that there is no economic obstacle to marriage, that child care is not a problem, and that the short duration of "puppy love" in society is due to the thousand conspiracies of a poorly organized society.

Consequently, adolescent sex is a problem in many cultures but not in Walden Two, where the young adult is allowed an honorable and satisfactory expression of natural feelings.

Frazier states that young girls have babies easily and that, generally, they are through with childbearing by their early twenties and, freed of the sole responsibility of child care, they are at liberty to pursue interesting lives.

It is significant to note that Skinner, through Frazier, says that at the end of her childbearing norm, the woman "is then quite on a par with men. She has made the special contribution which is either the duty or the privilege of women and can now take her place without dinstinction of sex. You may have noticed the complete equality of men and women among us." In fact, this statement suggests that a childbearing woman is not on a par with men and that to bear children is either her duty or must be regarded as a privilege, both of which are limited points of view. This does not allow for the woman who does not wish to have children and who does not define herself in terms of her ability to give birth. To say that a woman may take her place without distinction of sex seems to imply that to be distinctively female is negative. Furthermore, we have not been given evidence that complete equality exists between men and women in Walden Two, Frazier's statements to the contrary.

Frazier goes on to explain both the romantic and the scientific details of marriage in Walden Two; as usual, he counters all arguments skillfully. One of the curious statements Frazier makes in response to a question about birth control is that "we need to expand the culture which recognizes the need for birth control. . . . We don't worry about our birth rate or its consequences." This statement is an example of the phenomenon known as Doublespeak, a term taken from Orwell's *1984*.

When asked about genetic experiments, Frazier replies that this will be possible as the family structure weakens. This sensitive topic is attacked by Castle, who again tries to discredit Walden Two.

In Chapter 17, Frazier opens up the controversial topic of the importance of the family. He views the problem of the family from a detached, scientific point of view and takes a pragmatic attitude that what is good is whatever helps us survive, and that if the family is counter-productive to the aims of the larger society, then the family must be dispensed with. However, when Frazier describes the family as "an ancient form of community," he obscures the fact that "family" has meant many different things at different times; thus he leaves himself open to the charge that the family is not an integral part of human society, as is evidenced by tradition.

In fact, the nuclear family, as we think of it today, is a relatively recent phenomenon which has replaced the extended families and tribal families of the past. These changes were due to an increasingly industrialized, less agrarian life-style, and, therefore, we can see that the concept of family does change with the needs of individuals and society. When seen in this light, the family is more easily understood as a temporary, practical arrangement than as a sacred, inviolable, time-honored institution.

Castle and Frazier discuss the dynamics of marital relationships and the experiments done by the psychologists at Walden Two to strengthen the bonds between husband and wife. Frazier assures the group that there is no more pre-marital and extra-marital sex in Walden Two than in any other society and that, in fact, there is probably less.

In spite of his earlier claims of equality, Frazier gives as an example of a mature relationship the following quotation: "When a man strikes up an acquaintance with a woman, he does not worry about failing to make advances, and the woman isn't hurt if advances aren't made." Walden Two has absorbed the sexism of the larger culture in its assumption that it is the man who pursues and the woman who accepts. Although we will talk later of the language of Skinner's work, it is interesting to note here that he shifts from the active voice when speaking of the man to the passive voice when speaking of the woman.

Since marriage outside Walden Two is based on economics, laws of inheritance, and assurance of care for dependent women and children, it might be pertinent to speculate on why such an outmoded institution is carried over into a progressive, egalitarian society such as Walden Two.

Frazier returns to the discussion of child care in the community, declaring that communal child care eases the burden of the individual parent, allows the childless to participate in the process of child-raising, and provides the child with a wealth of love and role models. This, in turn, eliminates feelings of insecurity in both children and adults. The subject of insecurity triggers Frazier into attacking the traditional marriage, saying that it feeds on the insecurity of the housewife who is treated as if her security depends on her usefulness to the other family members. He ends the chapter with the philosophical truism that "those who stand to gain most are always the hardest to convince." With that, everyone goes off to do his/her work.

Chapters 18-20

Chapter 18 takes up a discussion of ambivalence and choice and begins with the group reporting to the work desk again. Because the lounges are occupied, they cannot continue with window-washing, so Rodge, Steve, and Burris stack firewood while Castle and the women go off to do "lighter work." While the former are working, they discuss their own dreams, and the pros and cons of Walden Two. It is obvious from this dialogue that Rodge is struggling with his desire to become a part of Walden Two, and with an equally strong desire to maintain his relationship with Barbara, who finds the whole idea of Walden Two outrageous. Rodge and Burris discuss the necessity of the social conscience and the lack of it in Barbara. After their work is finished and they have lunch, Burris goes off by himself to survey the art of Walden Two. Sitting down after an hour, he naps and is awakened by a group of people entering the lounge. Late for dinner, he rushes into the Swedish Room to find his group in the midst of a conversation centering around his absence. As dinner continues, the conversation takes a more serious turn as they discuss the failure of small communities of the past. Frazier becomes angry at Burris's drawing parallels between earlier attempts of utopian communities and Walden Two. He argues that Walden Two makes use of psychological studies and control conditions that were unknown to earlier communities, some of which were based on religious principles not shared by Walden Two.

In Chapter 20, the discussion continues from the roof of the common rooms after dinner is finished. Frazier asks Castle if he has taught ethics and if he can define the "Good Life." Castle admits that in spite of having taught courses in ethics, he cannot tell "what the Good Life consists of." Frazier offers to explain it to him. First, the Good Life consists of good health. Second, "an absolute minimum of unpleasant labor is part of the Good Life." He then re-emphasizes how Walden Two has virtually eliminated unpleasant work. Third, "the Good Life also means a chance to exercise talents and abilities." At Walden Two, members are encouraged to pursue all of their talents, arts, and other inclinations. And finally, "the Good Life means relaxation and rest." There is plenty of time for both in Walden Two. Frazier concludes: "And that's all, Mr. Castle — absolutely all. I can't give you a rational justification for any of it. I can't reduce it to any principle of 'the greatest good.' This is the Good Life. We know it. It's a fact, not a theory." Thus, the Good Life consists largely in living it rather than theorizing about it.

Frazier also says that in order to keep the Good Life in operation, all that is needed is "adequate behavioral engineering," and that the only problem here is with the members who come to Walden Two as adults. Castle still objects that the Good Life, as explained, only encourages living from day to day. Frazier counters that most people do prefer to live from day to day, and if there is a person who desires to contemplate long-range goals and plans, there is nothing in Walden Two that would hinder him/her from doing so.

Castle then objects that a person who desires to make great contributions to society for either fortune or fame would be stifled. Frazier counters this by pointing out that there is no need for great fortunes at Walden Two and points out that the exceptional abilities of one person must then force one to reveal the more limited abilities of others and that this is wrong. At Walden Two if a person does poorly in an assigned job, he/she is not blamed; instead, he/she is simply given a new type of job that fits his/her temperament better. As Castle still objects, maintaining that the members of the community don't understand the moral or ethical implications of what their life means, Frazier counters by saying that Walden Two is a living example of a community "in which there's no crime and very few petty lapses," and that this alone is sufficient to attest to the success of the community. They then retire for the night.

Chapters 21-22

In Chapter 21, Burris decides to take a walk, have a cigarette, and digest the information he has just heard. He notices that very few people smoke at Walden Two and that his own interest in tobacco has lessened. Pondering this, he meets Steve and Mary, who ask for his opinion of Walden Two; they admit that they are thinking of joining. They are overwhelmed with the kind of life that the community offers them in comparision to the life that they would return to outside of Walden Two.

Steve and Mary leave Burris and look forward to the next day when they can discuss their plans with Frazier. The discussion awakens within Burris uncomfortable feelings of conflict. Unable to reconcile his practical nature with what he considers to be his foolish dreams, he goes to sleep.

In Chapter 22, we find Castle smugly asserting that the community is a hoax. Castle is so overbearing in his manner and so overstates his case that Burris cannot take him seriously. The breakfast conversation centers around Steve and Mary's decision to join Walden Two. It is obvious that Rodge and Barbara have been arguing over the same issue. When Steve and Mary join the group for breakfast, they inform Burris that they have yet to pass the medical examination, the final barrier to their being admitted. As the two leave for their medical examination with Mr. Meyerson, the rest go to work and finish the window-washing job. At noon, Mr. Meyerson treats the group to a tour of the medical center. He stresses the importance of preventive medicine and introduces the group to Miss Ely, the dentist. We are told that because of the extraordinary good health of the inhabitants, much time is spent in the laboratory perfecting methods of prevention. Burris is impressed with the system but Castle insists that the doctors of Walden Two are taking advantage of the state's medical schools and prepares to challenge Frazier on that subject.

Chapters 23-24

After the tour of the medical center, Frazier asks the group for their impressions of Walden Two. They make a proper acknowledgement of the success of Walden Two. Frazier points out to them the single most incredible fact about Walden Two is the mere fact that it *does* exist at this particular time and in this particular place. All other utopias have existed either in some far away place or in some far away time. Frazier points out: "Why 'Utopia' is the Greek for 'nowhere' and Butler spelled 'nowhere' backwards! Bacon chose lost Atlantis, and Shangri-La is cut off by the highest mountains in the world. Bellamy and Morris felt it necessary to get away by a century or two in the dimension of time." But Frazier points out that Walden Two exists presently and "the Good Life is waiting for us — here and now!"

When Castle questions the practicality of setting up a new way of life that conflicts with government and politics, Frazier answers him by making an important distinction between politics that support a government and the "non-politics" of Walden Two. Although he does not say so, the distinction he is making is really between reform politics and radical politics. He says explicitly, "you can't make progress toward the Good Life by political action! Not under any current form of government!" His only concession to government as it exists currently is to vote in all of the local issues for practical purposes. A Political Manager is responsible for studying the various local issues, and then issuing the "Walden Two ticket," which instructs all of the members of Walden Two how to vote. They then all vote the straight Walden Two ticket. In this manner, the community is able to sway elections for their own purposes. People of similar interests in other communities look to the Walden Two ticket for advice on voting. Castle objects that the "members merely vote as they are told." Frazier responds: "And why not? Do you think we'd be so foolish as to vote half one way and half the other? We might as well stay home. Remember that our interests are all alike, and our Political Manager is in the best possible position to tell us what candidates will act in those interests."

The discussion moves on to the question of religion in Walden Two. Frazier explains that Walden Two differs from other utopias in that it wasn't founded because of religious convictions, and that no religious instruction is given to the children, although the parents may teach the children anything they like. The founding philosophy of Walden Two is very much a part of the twentieth century, as it is based on scientific principles and situational ethics. Frazier says that religious practices have fallen by the wayside along with drinking and smoking. There *is*, however, a Sunday meeting with a rather eclectic program consisting of music, philosophy, poetry, and the like, which serves as a kind of group therapy. Frazier says there is no need here for the mystical or supernatural, and the care that churches sometimes provide for the old and infirm are unnecessary in a community that watches out for the interests of all of its members. For the sake of public relations, however, a clergyman is invited once a year to attend a Sunday service, and since he is promised a good meal, the clergyman always accepts. In this way they quell rumors that might circulate outside about the community and continue to maintain good relations with the outside world.

Castle worries that the people of Walden Two are concerned with their own particular interests and are not contributing any efforts towards achieving world peace. Frazier points out simply that any civilization that does not declare wars or contribute to standing armies and makes no attempt at imperialism is contributing to world peace.

Chapter 24 deals with other communities and social conscience. Burris asks if it isn't difficult to keep the young people from leaving Walden Two because of the allure of the outside world. Frazier answers that while they do not propagandize or make unfavorable comparisons between the outside world and Walden Two that the children develop a social conscience much earlier than most and see the direct cause-and-effect relationship between wealth and competitiveness, and poverty. Again, a comparison between other communities and Walden Two comes up, but Frazier dismisses their attempts at change as feeble. He says that communities such as the Amish communities and monasteries have been left behind by the modern world and cannot offer their members the advantages of Walden Two. In addition, other communities propagandize and lose their members because of intellectual stultification. Walden Two is so "naturally satisfying" that no indoctrination is necessary.

Chapters 25-27

Chapter 25 is an examination of the people of Walden Two. Suspicious that Frazier may have arranged what he wants the newcomers to see at Walden Two, Burris decides to wander about and scrutinize the people at random. He observes several different groups and finds them to be good-natured and cordial. A group of women draw him into their conversation and begin asking questions about the academic world and the standardization of students. Burris finds these questions difficult to answer. As politely as possible, he leaves and eventually discovers a concert. As the concert ends, the pianist jumps to his feet and it turns out to be Frazier, who notices Burris. The chapter ends as the two walk off together.

In Chapter 26, on his way back to his room, Burris is able to talk with a member of Walden Two. As he begins talking to an older woman, he recognizes that he has been searching desperately for something wrong with Walden Two. As they talk, he discovers in her a quiet serenity that confirms for him that Walden Two works. He asks her about Frazier, but it is obvious that she knows him only by sight and does not conceive of him as a leader or messiah.

Burris takes his leave and goes to his room, where he is once again embroiled in inner turmoil. He has to admit that Walden Two is everything that Frazier had promised, and this realization unnerves him. The chapter ends with Burris throwing open the door of his room, frustrated that Frazier knows what he is up to. He says "Frazier was not there, but I fancied I smelled brimstone." We have referred to the religious symbolism and the fact that Frazier will later liken himself to Christ. Here, in this image, Burris compares Frazier to Satan, who tempts him with a diabolical plan. Burris is worried that if he accepts Frazier's offer of the "Good Life" that he will be "selling his soul" in the bargain.

Chapter 27 opens with the discovery by Castle and Burris that other Waldens exist. In fact, there are at least four, in addition to Walden Two. The name of the community is based on a pun of Thoreau's *Walden*, which is Walden One: Walden Two can thus be understood as "all this and Walden, too."

To maintain a representative cross-section of individuals, and to lessen the chance of dangerous inbreeding, the communities occasionally subdivide and members move to other Waldens. Burris asks if members who are taken in from the outside create any problems for the community because of their different backgrounds and social conditions, especially in their sexual attitudes. Frazier says that community psychology and peer pressure take care of any disturbances.

Frazier sees the future as consisting of the absorption of the outside society into the expanding communities of Walden. Castle likens Frazier's plans for the future to Nazism, and the debate between the two men grows hot. Frazier's rather paternalistic notion of improvement is met with

Castle's rejoinder, "O brave new world, indeed!" This is an allusion to Huxley's *Brave New World,* in which an individualist goes mad when faced with the mindless conformity of a future society. Castle charges that Frazier is a dictator, and Frazier points out that any of the individuals at Walden Two are free to leave any time they want to. Burris comes to Frazier's defense by mentioning the woman he met who could hardly identify Frazier when his name was mentioned; consequently, there is no one dominant figure at Walden Two, whereas in a dictatorship, the country is controlled with an iron hand by one all-powerful figure or dictator. In fact, Frazier maintains, "a society which functions for the good of all cannot tolerate the emergence of individual figures." For this reason, there are no great single leaders or "great athletes," and there is no hero worship. Even the study of history is not taught because history has been controlled too often by great individuals and reflects the values of a society that Walden Two does not respect. The discussion ends amiably and they go off.

Chapters 28-29

In Chapter 28, Castle and Burris discuss the previous evening's conversation and Castle brings up the fact that Frazier has hedged on several points, such as dignity, integrity, and democracy, points that he and many others would find important in any discussion of an ideal society. They leave for the dining room, where they are joined by the rest of the group. Frazier has put on his best manners, to which Barbara responds with a series of questions, coquettish glances, and pouts, all behavior that Frazier regards as the typical behavior of women raised in competitive cultures. Nevertheless, he responds to her flirtatiousness to the point that he is flustered.

After breakfast, the group wanders around aimlessly while they wait for the Sunday service to begin. They engage in desultory conversation and reassemble for the service, but Frazier and Burris depart in order to talk between themselves. Frazier asks Burris about Rogers and Barbara. Burris admits that Rogers is intrigued by Walden Two, but that he is torn between his attachment to Barbara and his dream of a utopian idea.

As the two go to Frazier's room, the conversation begins to center on Frazier himself. Burris is surprised by Frazier's sloppiness and disorder. Frazier asks Burris not to penalize Walden Two for the personal dislike that Burris might feel towards Frazier. He explains that not having been raised in Walden Two, he is not a good example of what the community intends to do or can do. He admits that his emotions get out of control and that he has been warped by the culture from which he came. However, he has done what he can to engineer the type of society that will produce the healthy individual that he will never be.

This section is the first in which we see Frazier admitting his shortcomings and begging Burris not to dismiss the community by confusing Frazier's faults with any real or imagined flaws in the community. This chapter represents a turning point in the book. One of the ways to enlist support for an argument is to evoke sympathy in the reader. For all of his heavy handedness and insensitivity, Frazier here evokes more sympathy from the reader than he does at any other point in the book. At a time when Burris is struggling with what he knows to be true intellectually and what he feels emotionally, this interlude could serve as a piece of behavioral engineering designed to make Burris feel more generously toward Frazier and toward Walden Two.

Chapter 29 sets the stage for another confrontation between Castle and Frazier. Although plans had been made for an afternoon outing, a storm forces them to call off their plans. The young couples go off, leaving Castle, Frazier, and Burris to clear up the questions so far left unanswered. Castle begins with an accusation designed to open a conclusive verbal battle between himself and Frazier, but Frazier, always the manipulator of behavior, turns Castle's ferocity to his own advantage and manages to make him look foolish. Castle has decided that even though Frazier has a less active role presently as community leader, that Frazier had certainly been in control during the founding stages of Walden Two and had engineered the community to conform to his wishes without his overt manipulation. Castle admits that the community is efficient, but in the same way that an anthill or a beehive is efficient. He feels that the freedom of humankind has been replaced with a kind of complacent instinctiveness. Frazier argues on the one hand that he is not one of the "powers that be," and, on the other, that since it is the majority that is scrabbling about like so many crabs, it is up to the minority who understand the science of behavior to put humankind back on the road toward fulfillment and achievement. Frazier argues that since the tools and techniques of behavioral engineering do exist that it is a kindness to utilize them for the benefit of mankind rather than letting them fall prey to manipulators with less noble motives. Castle states that he would "dump your science of behavior in the ocean" and allow humanity its freedom of choice. The conflict here is between two opposing points of view that takes us back to the age-old discussion of free will and determinism. Of course, Frazier and by extension, Skinner, as a behaviorist, does not believe in a concept of free will. The foundation of the behaviorist theory rests on the assumption that all behaviors are learned and can be predicted and elicited. Although Castle is arguing on behalf of our freedom and basic integrity, by this time, through others' descriptions of him as engineered by Skinner, he has been made to look so pitiful and ridiculous that the others and the readers may dismiss his arguments in the face of Frazier's and Burris's cooler logic.

In one of his most convincing tirades, Frazier talks about the control demonstrated by sales people, advertisers, and educators in influencing our choices in everyday life and says that we must counteract those influences with a better system of control than that of those less scrupulous than ourselves. What Frazier never says explicitly is who will be in control. His use of "we" at times may deceive the reader into believing that it refers to the community as a whole and that everyone will have a say in who is controlled and by whom and according to what standards. In fact, only those people well-trained in the subtleties of behavioral psychology would be able to use the techniques on others. We know from the discussion in Chapter 10 that the Dairy Manager does not understand the basic principles of behavioral engineering, but is concerned only with his specific duties. We are not told who educates the children or if behavioral psychology is taught at all. Who, then, might practice behavioral engineering? We must remember that Frazier is a psychologist, and it is in his hands that this powerful instrument lies. Castle argues against the basic premise of behavioristic psychology and, thereby, leaves himself open to a charge of ignorance in the face of the evidence we now have of consumers being manipulated by the media. What in fact he should be arguing is the question of who will control and how, but since Skinner has pre-determined the questions and arguments against his theory, he has been able to make his reader feel as if all the pertinent questions have been answered when the reader's attention has, in reality, been diverted away from the most significant question.

Frazier then maneuvers Castle into a pointless argument about democracy and Frazier finally admits that Walden Two and other communities like it will be successful in part because behavioral engineering can make its members feel a sense of personal freedom that does not really exist.

The chapter ends with Frazier carefully pointing out the differences between the practices of Walden Two and the practices of communism as it exists in places like Russia (to which Castle has compared Walden Two). Frazier sees four things wrong with Russia: 1) The decline in the experimental spirit; 2) the heavy indoctrination that Russia must employ to hold its members; 3) the encouragement of hero worship; and 4) its basis in power and its dependence on maintaining that power. Frazier dismisses all of Castle's arguments with a shrug of the shoulders.

Chapters 30-32

As Chapter 29 ends with the statement that Frazier has "had enough of Castle's 'general issues,' " so Chapter 30 begins with Burris's statement: "And so had I." While Burris agrees with Castle that Frazier shies away from generalities, he feels that Walden Two was founded on "specific behavioral and cultural laws and techniques." Suddenly, the storm outside subsides and, metaphorically, for Burris, the community springs to life. The three move through the community. Everywhere they look there are signs of the complete success of Walden Two. It can be seen on the faces of the inhabitants. Frazier leaves them abruptly and they agree to meet for suppper.

After dinner, the group breaks up, and Castle and Burris walk along together. Burris suspects that Castle's good mood is due to some dismissal of Frazier and his methods as fascist. In fact, this is the case. As Burris and Castle argue, Burris finds himself pigeonholing Castle. In order to escape from a discussion that he is sick of, Burris suggests that they go back to their room and listen to a symphony by Mozart being piped through a loud speaker. As Castle settles down to grading papers, Burris finds that he is confused and indecisive about his own future. He considers the simple choice of Steve and Mary, the struggles of Rodge, and his own unsatisfying academic life. In an attempt to take his mind off the entire situation, he tries to remember all of the poetry that he has ever learned, but what comes to him are the lines of a verse admonishing him that time is rushing on and that if he is to make a satisfying life, he must decide now about how to do so.

In Chapter 32, we shall see Burris being won over when Frazier offers the challenge that Burris needs to accept the community. As the chapter begins, Castle and the others (with the exception of Steve and Mary) are preparing to leave. Burris is disgusted with Castle's views about Walden Two, and he dismisses him and his arguments from consideration.

Frazier attempts to get Burris off by himself, and Burris is glad to comply. As Frazier goes about his work for the day, he reopens the discussion of Walden Two and Burris's feelings about it. Putting personal antagonisms aside, Burris compliments Frazier on his experiment in living and admits that he envies Frazier the chance to do something meaningful and worthwhile.

The one thing that has been bothering Burris is that it would seem that there is nothing left to be done in Walden Two. Burris states that what is needed to make these experiments in improving the lives of humankind is financial endowment, a sufficient challenge to hold the interest of talented people, and extensive research. Frazier laughs and exclaims that Burris's specifications "are precisely those of Walden Two." Burris is stunned. Frazier talks at length about the challenge of the future and what remains to be done with communities like Walden Two. In one of the most famous and oft-quoted passages, Frazier turns the tide with these words: "What remains to be done? . . . Well, what do you say to the design of personalities? Would that interest you? The control of temperament? Give me the specifications, and I'll give you the man! What do you say to the control of motivation, building the interests which will make men most productive and most successful? Does that seem to you fantastic? Yet some of the techniques are available, and more can be worked out experimentally. Think of the possibilities! A society in which there is no failure, no boredom, no duplication of effort!"

Frazier continues in the same vein, hitting every weak point in Burris's defense and offering him the challenge of a lifetime. Burris gets no chance in this chapter to reply.

Chapters 33-36

Having left the room, Frazier leads Burris through a woods and up to a mossy bank where it is obvious that Frazier has often sat. Taking out a small telescope, Frazier surveys all that is Walden Two and comments on the members that he can see from this vantage point. In a joking manner, he makes several references to biblical aphorisms. He then lies down in such a manner as to suggest the crucifixion. Burris is frightened and uncomfortable and makes a remark designed to elicit reassurrance from Frazier that he does not see himself as a kind of god. To Burris's dismay, Frazier points out the similarity between himself and God. Burris finally stops him with a charge of blasphemy. Frazier suggests that they change the metaphor but stick with the facts of Walden Two and his place in it. The analogy between God and Frazier comes up again, however, and Burris notes that Frazier speaks of Jesus as if He were an "honored colleague." In an emotional outburst, Frazier refers to the members of Walden Two as his children and he says: "I love them."

This chapter is the culmination of all the religious allusions and metaphors that have gone before in other chapters. The God/Frazier analogy is a strong one, and one might question the efficacy of substituting an old god with a new one. Nevertheless, Frazier is again depicted here at his most human, and though it is not stated until later, Burris has pretty much made his decision about joining Walden Two.

In Chapter 35, the leavetaking begins. Frazier's friendly goodby to Castle embarrasses the man, and Castle responds awkwardly. We are not told of Burris's feelings as he leaves Walden Two. What follows in this chapter is the description of the journey back and the final goodby to Steve and Mary, who have accompanied them part way. Burris feels a great need to be alone, and when Castle later engages him in a discussion, he finds himself ready with answers that Frazier himself might have given. Burris sees Castle as being enormously self-deluded and realizes that Frazier is a far superior person.

At the first opportunity, Burris takes off to settle the question of Walden Two in his own mind. Everything he sees during his walk convinces him that Frazier is right. His position as an educator has taught him to question the assumptions of a culture, and he understands at last that in the little time that he has left in this world, that there is only one way to make it worthwhile. He decides to return to Walden Two. Settling on a march as the only honest way to return to Walden Two, he begins to walk. At last he is inspired, feeling as if a future really does lay ahead.

Chapter 36 begins rather abruptly with Burris and Frazier discussing how the book should end. We discover that Burris has written the book at the request of the Office of Information as a kind of report, or human-interest story, on his decision to join the community. Frazier urges Burris to be explicit about the ending, as he imagines all the alternative endings that others could supply which would change the outcome altogether. Burris tells us what the future holds for him now, and we see his life to be as complete and as fulfilled as he has so earnestly hoped. He recounts his arrival (this time for good) at Walden Two, and his welcome from Steve, who informs him that Frazier had told him Burris would be back. Burris reacts with dismay at his own predictability and then laughs. The chapter ends with a paraphrase of Browning's lines from *Pippa Passes*, ("God's in his heaven. All's right with the World."), which reads "Frazier was not in his heaven. All was right with the world." This reassures Burris and us that the community is not to be feared, and that emotional resistance is trivial and should be put aside. The book then ends satisfactorily and on a cheerful note which suggests that all have made the right decisions for themselves and that Burris's decision is at least as valid as, say, Castle's or Rodge's.

The argument of which Castle and Frazier represented opposite points of view has been resolved in the synthesis of common sense and open-mindedness that is represented by Burris.

ESTABLISHED UTOPIAN COMMUNITIES

The utopian spirit as we have been discussing it is revealed through the written words of men who were critical of the world they lived in and dreamers of a better world. What we cannot forget is that there have been many instances of groups of people who believed so strongly in the possibility of improving their lot that they attempted to found new communities planned according to their ideal principles. Basically, this is what Frazier has done, and this is what Rogers and Steve Jamnik are seeking. That is, Frazier has not written books about utopians; instead, he has established one at Walden Two. Invariably such an undertaking in the past has required a move from the "old country" that they found intolerable to a new, open territory. For this reason, America of the nineteenth century furnished admirable opportunities, and there were scores of such group settlements throughout the United States and Canada — large and small, successful and abortive. Some of these communities have endured through a good many generations, particularly those based on religious principles: the Mennonites, the Amish, and the Dunkards.

Fourierism exerted a wide influence on the United States in the 1830s and 1840s. The author of the doctrines was Charles Fourier, who wrote *Traité de l'Association Domestique Agricole* (1822) and *Le Nouveau Monde Industriel* (1829). The leader of the movement in America was Albert Brisbane. An influential convert was Horace Greeley. Of the numerous communities, the most famous was Brook Farm, which attracted the attention of Hawthorne, Emerson, Margaret Fuller, and members of the Alcott family. An interesting plan for such a community was discussed quite seriously by Coleridge and Robert Southey, to be called a "pantisocracy" but it did not materialize. A more practical group established a settlement at New Harmony, Indiana, under the leadership of a Scottish industrialist named Robert Owen. A second French utopianist, Etienne Cabet, after writing a utopian novel entitled *Le Voyage en Icarie* (1840), established his own community — first in Texas, then later in Nauvoo, Illinois. Other successful communities deserving special mention are the Oneida (N.Y.) Community; the Shakers, in 1840, with villages in eight states; the Amana Community, still thriving in Iowa; and the Hutterites, with communities from the Dakotas through western Canada. In modern Israel, the communal settlements *(kibbutzim)* operate on principles and under regulations closely resembling those described in Skinner's *Walden Two*.

No two communities were identical in purpose and operation, but certain aspects of the utopian norm appear frequently. Many of them followed the plan of community of property, equality in sharing labor, community rearing of children, simplicity and uniformity of dress, avoidance of luxury, rigid codes of behavior, pacifism, and a government by selected elders. All of this is similar to Frazier's Walden Two.

UTOPIA AND COMMUNISM

There is a tendency to dodge the term "communism" when discussing any utopian plan, no doubt because of the antipathy that has developed in association with the term, particularly in America, where a large majority of people view communism as our most real threat. The fact remains that many utopian societies are closely aligned with a communist society. Skinner, writing in 1947, carefully avoided associating the Walden Two society with communism even though such great utopias of the past, (such as More's) were essentially communistic societies. In fact, Frazier, at the end of Chapter 30, gives four objections to Russian communism: 1) the decline in the experimental spirit; 2) the heavy indoctrination that Russia must employ to hold its members; 3) the encouragement of hero worship; and 4) its basis in power and its dependence on maintaining that power.

The first meaning of "communism," according to *The American Heritage Dictionary,* is: "A social system characterized by the absence of classes and by common ownership of the means of production and subsistence." Accordingly, Walden Two can be classed as communistic, and the same can be said of a majority of those works described as "utopian literature." Established communities that have been labeled as utopian were also, in most instances, communistic, despite the fact that some of them were founded with a religious emphasis, like the Amish community, some with a rational and philanthropic motivation, like Brook Farm, and others with no particular emphasis on religion, like Walden Two.

A misunderstanding arises from the fact that in the English-speaking world it has become customary to refer to the governments of Russia, China, and their satellites as the Communist countries. However, the so-called communism of Russia and China is officially and properly called socialism. That is their own term: the Union of Soviet Socialist Republics. At any rate, calling any utopia and the USSR both communistic could give the reader an erroneous impression. A comparison of the Soviet system with the true communism of a utopian society reveals numerous basic differences. At the core of a utopian system is community of property and services and the elimination of money and commerce. None of those features is characteristic of the Russian/Chinese system. And for another important difference, note that the kind of democracy practiced in a utopia is not accepted in the totalitarian Soviet states. The different approaches to religion reinforce the necessity for sharply separating the two types of society. Religion, while it does not play a major role in Walden Two, is available to all members and certain religious teachings are often used for many purposes.

The obvious conclusion is that it is perfectly correct to call utopians Communists, but it is a serious blunder to identify their type of society with the Socialist forms of government that we think of as representing communism in the modern world.

ANTI-UTOPIAS

A body of writing commonly associated with the utopian tradition, even though the works seem to be in direct contradiction, are variously referred to as anti-utopian or distopian. This group includes some distinguished books which B. F. Skinner assumes that the reader is familiar with. The books that Skinner (or some character in *Walden Two*) most often refers to are Samuel Butler's *Erewhon,* Aldous Huxley's *Brave New World,* and George Orwell's *1984.* Terms such as Doublespeak, BIG BROTHER, and phrases such as "Oh, brave new world" are frequently mentioned in the conversations at Walden Two. Therefore, an examination of the basic ideas of each work will further illuminate *Walden Two.*

If it is remembered that the primary motivation for all utopian writing is a desire to attack the ills of an existing society (or a feeling of dissatisfaction with the existing society as felt by Steve and Rogers), we will recognize that these anti-utopian documents are not entirely remote from the traditional utopias. Indeed, the anti-utopian works purport to offer utopian solutions to social, economic, and political problems at the outset, but sooner or later — usually sooner — the reader discovers that the author's real purpose is satirical. In *Walden Two*, Frazier often mentions some aspects of these works and assures the reader that the Walden Two community will not be trapped into falling into the same type of situation as described by one of the above authors.

Samuel Butler's *Erewhon*

The title of Samuel Butler's *Erewhon* (1872) is intended as an anagram for "nowhere," and that, it is recalled, is a loose translation for "utopia" — no place or no where.

Unlike Walden Two, Erewhon is a remote kingdom, not on any map, which the narrator claims to have discovered in his travels. This setting aligns *Erewhon* with earlier types of utopias rather than with *Walden Two*. Much of the landscape resembles New Zealand, where Butler lived for a few years, as Walden Two resembles places where Skinner lived. The residents of Erewhon are without contact with other nations and live according to their own eccentric patterns of civilization. In many respects their lives resemble that of contemporary Western civilization rather than Plato's or More's societies. They are governed by a monarchy and have lawyers, judges, and prisons. They have money, banks, rich citizens and poor ones.

The features of Erewhonian society that surprise the author are those that differ from the England that he knew. According to the early impressions of the travelers, the people all appear to be exceptionally healthy, exceedingly handsome, and altogether contented. Their life-style is characterized by simplicity and gracious manners, best described as Arcadian. Gradually, however, oddities, or what appear to be oddities to the visitor, begin to surface. Duplicity pervades every aspect of thought and action. The natives habitually profess agreement to a proposition although they do not believe in it, and their friends are perfectly aware that they do not mean what they say. There are two separate banking systems in operation and two sets of religions. The people give lip service to what they call the Musical Banks, but they transact all serious business with the currency of the other chain of banks. Similarly, they recognize a group of dieties representing the personification of human qualities — justice, hope, love, fear — and erect statues to them; but their pragmatic morality is evidently dictated by a goddess, Ydgrun (Grundy). More and more they reveal themselves to the traveler as victims of self-deception and inverted logic. Their universities are called Colleges of Unreason, and the principal course of study is Hypothetics.

One of the most eccentric features of Erewhonian life is the interpretation of crime and punishment. Illness, for example, is treated as a crime. (In *Walden Two*, Frazier explains that if someone is incapable of performing an assigned task, or fails at something, one would not punish that person any more than if he/she had an illness.) Sentences of varying degrees of severity are pronounced according to the nature and seriousness of the disease. There are no physicians in the country. Those actions which Europeans consider criminal — theft, fraud, embezzlement — are regarded as weaknesses of character deserving sympathy and help, help which is provided through the ministrations of "straighteners."

Another surprising feature is the attitude toward machinery. Several centuries earlier, the Erewhonians had attained a remarkable stage of sophistication in the development of machinery, but through the teachings of a prophet they had been persuaded that machines might someday become masters over men, with the result that they destroyed all of the machinery having any degree of complexity and outlawed any further experimentation in the field. They retained only the simplest kinds of implements — spades and scythes — and horses and wagons. (In *Walden Two*, Frazier assures the visitors that they have not returned to this type of utopian atavism; quite the contrary, they utilize every type of modern machine.)

The reader, following the narrator's shifting attitude from admiration to surprise and finally to contempt, is led to believe that the author is bent on demonstrating the vast inferiority of the Erewhonians to his fellow Englishmen; but it gradually becomes clear that he attributes to Englishmen much of the irrationality and the ingenious equivocations that make the Erewhonians look foolish. The difference is only one of degree. Thus, Butler's *Erewhon* is close to being a satire, such as that found in portions of Swift's *Gulliver's Travels*.

Aldous Huxley's *Brave New World*

Huxley's *Brave New World* (1932) offers a projection of what life on earth might become in another five hundred years if technology plays an increasingly dominant role and if government control of all aspects of human activity becomes absolute. Skyscrapers will become taller, factories will become more efficient, travel will be mainly by air, diseases will be virtually eliminated, and universal happiness will be provided through elaborate sports and entertainment programs and through a happiness pill called *soma*.

Most radical of the anti-utopian features is the denial of equality. People will be classified in a caste system that is achieved through controlled genetics that insures the society of a supply of dull-witted, underdeveloped individuals to perform the less agreeable jobs and those demanding lesser skills. In *Walden Two*, it will be remembered, the less agreeable jobs are given higher labor credits so as to make the job less unpleasant.

The application of scientific methods begins in the "Central London Hatchery and Conditioning Centre." There, humans are bred in test tubes, transferred later to larger jars, and nourished under controlled conditions until they reach the stage for hatching or "decanting." Even in the test tube stage, they are marked for treatment that will produce the type of human being desired. The types are labelled alpha, beta, gamma, delta, and epsilon, with certain plus or minus grades within each type. In infancy, the individuals are scientifically "conditioned" to cultivate certain desires, to abhor certain things, and to believe certain truisms, according to the kind of service for which they are designated. The conditioning takes the form of nutritional treatment, electric shock, screeching sirens, and hypnopaedia — that is, sleep-teaching.

Some critics of *Walden Two* maintain that the type of conditioning that is to take place through behavorial engineering might not differ philosophically from the type of genetic control in *Brave New World*. After all, Frazier did say: "Give me your specifications, and I'll give you the man!" (Chapter 32).

Every individual is employed according to his/her classification — in an office, a factory, a hatchery, on a farm, or flying a helicopter taxi. A great variety of entertainment is provided for after-working hours — sports like electromagnetic golf, Riemann-surface tennis, and centrifugal bumble-puppy. There are lively nightclubs and "feelies," movies that provide accompanying scents and that also stimulate appropriate tactile sensations. Every evening seems to end with sexual liaison. Sexual relations are completely promiscuous. "Everyone belongs to everyone" is one of the cliches drummed into one's consciousness through conditioning. There is no such thing as marriage. Contraceptives are provided by the government to make sure that people will not interfere with the test tube method of producing children. Sex is purely for sport.

Huxley's *Brave New World,* in which emotions and all feelings are controlled by *conditioning,* offers some frightening parallels to *Walden Two,* in which Frazier is going to create a society through *behavioral conditioning* "in which there is no failure, no boredom, no duplication of effort," a world in which the lives of the individuals are controlled: "Let us control the lives of our children and see what we can make of them." (Chapter 32).

George Orwell's *1984*

In George Orwell's *1984* (1949), the society of the year 1984, which Orwell projects for us, is based on the assumption that a "limited" nuclear war of the 1950s left civilization severely crippled and that government controls were seized by well-organized opportunists employing the familiar methods of a police state to maintain power. London, the scene of the novel's action, is the capital of Oceania, one of three superpowers. The other superpowers are called Eastasia and Eurasia.

Oceania is completely dominated by the members of "the Party," a handpicked group of loyal supporters of the government. The mass of the population, the proletariat or "proles," are purposely kept poor and ignorant and are without any voice in public affairs. Actually, the real power is held by the "Inner Party," the elite of the Party membership.

In *Walden Two,* even though there is no overt sense of a "power" running the community, Frazier and the "we" that he uses, do control the community: "Our members are practically always doing what they want to do — what they "choose" to do — but we see to it that they will want to do precisely the things which are best for themselves and the community. *Their behavior is determined,* yet they are free" (Chapter 33; italics ours).

In *1984,* the methods employed by the Party to maintain control and to manipulate the population are copied directly from the records of Nazi Germany and Stalinist Russia. Any opposition to the system in deed, word, or thought is summarily stamped out. Naturally, freedom of speech and of the press are suppressed. Spies are everywhere. There are hundreds of posters throughout the city showing the enormous head of a man with steely eyes and a heavy black mustache. The caption of the posters reads: BIG BROTHER IS WATCHING YOU. Monitoring screens for official spying are in public places, in hallways, and even in apartments. One's every action or word may be under surveillance. People live in constant fear of being detected committing some crime or of being suspected of some crime, and there is always present the dread of a banging on the door in the middle of the night. Confessions are wrested even from innocent persons by refined methods of torture.

A new form of language called "Newspeak" is being developed to facilitate the process of thought control, and there is a movement called "Doublethink," whereby the most absurd ambiguities are propounded in all seriousness. The mottoes of the Party are: "War is Peace," "Freedom is Slavery," and "Ignorance is Strength." The Ministry of Truth deals mainly with propaganda, the Ministry of Peace manages military operations, the Ministry of Love is concerned with matters of law and order, and the Ministry of Plenty regulates the economy.

1984 is brutally anti-utopian in every detail, the complete antithesis of the meliorative societies conceived of by More, Bellamy, Morris and others. Like *Walden Two*, they are all cast in novel form with a plot line and cast of characters. And even though Frazier often asserts the contrary, the reader must determine if *Walden Two* possesses certain elements of the anti-utopian society.

THOREAU'S *WALDEN* AND SKINNER'S *WALDEN TWO*

Skinner takes his title from Thoreau's *Walden* and as Frazier explains, "Walden Two" means a second Walden, and also "Walden too." Thoreau's *Walden* is a record of Thoreau's move from society to Walden Pond, where he attempted to reduce his needs to the barest essentials of life and to establish an intimate, spiritual relationship with nature. Likewise, Steve and Rogers are also dissatisfied with society and they seek Walden Two as an alternative life-style.

For Thoreau, living at Walden Pond was a noble experiment in basically three ways. First, Thoreau was intent upon resisting the debilitating effects of the industrial revolution with its division of labor, the mind-dulling repetition of factory work, and a materialistic vision of life. The Walden Pond experiment allowed Thoreau to "turn back the clock" to the simpler, agrarian way of life that was quickly disappearing in New England. *Walden Two*, then, advocates a return to a basically agrarian way of life and a rejection of a purely materialistic way of life. Second, by reducing his expenditures, Thoreau reduced the time necessary to support himself; he could then devote more time to the perfection of his life and his art. At Walden Two, one of the main emphases is upon the reduced amount of time that the individual must work — the work day at Walden Two has been reduced to a four-hour work day. Third, Thoreau asserted that one can most easily experience the Ideal (or the Divine) through nature; at Walden Pond, Thoreau was able to test continually the validity of this theory by living closely, day-to-day, with nature.

Thoreau also believed that once we critically review our lives, we will immediately discover a major hindrance to personal growth and happiness: the blind acceptance of traditional, conventional ways of living as handed down by previous generations. We should not be tied down by society's definition of ourselves or of life, but should confront life in a new, fresh way. By discarding those values of society which are worthless and sometimes dehumanizing, individuals would be able to discover life's meaning for themselves. Thoreau maintains that the most dehumanizing of our traditional values is the emphasis placed on property and maintains that one is wealthy in relationship to the amount of things that one can do without. Property is an encumbrance to freedom. The citizenry of Walden Two are certainly searching for a new way of life and have abandoned all claims to owning property.

In the final analysis, however, Thoreau's aims were significantly different from Skinner's aims in *Walden Two*. Unlike Skinner, whose behaviorial engineering would structure people's lives, Thoreau emphasizes the importance of the complete individuality of each person. Thoreau believes that once we discover what is within us, we should then construct a vision of how we can develop the potentiality for the greatness that we find. We can become whatever we choose to be. Our potential is vast and is capable of being realized in this life. Thoreau is convinced that "if one advances confidently in the direction of his dreams, and endeavors to live the life which he has imagined, he will meet with a success unexpected in common hours." (One of the emphases in Walden Two is to achieve a utopia, not in the distant future, but here and now.)

But whereas *Walden Two* implies the need of a certain degree of conformity or control, Thoreau believes that conformity is a trap to be completely avoided: "Why should we be in such desperate haste to succeed, and in such desperate enterprises? If a man does not keep pace with his companions, perhaps it is because he hears a different drummer. Let him step to the music he hears, however measured or far away." Inner exploration and growth are the personal concerns of each unique individual; each must discover his/her own truths and live by them accordingly. Thus, *Walden* ultimately concludes with an emphatic note of optimism and hope in humankind's ability to transcend its self-imposed limitations and fulfill its unmeasured potential for excellence. *Walden Two* ends with an emphasis on the predictability of human nature and a belief that regulation and control of human nature is necessary to achieve happiness and equality. Clearly, Thoreau and Skinner have very different notions of human nature and our hope for the future in spite of the similarity of the titles.

SINS OF OMISSION: RACISM AND SEXISM IN *WALDEN TWO*

From the beginning of *Walden Two,* we understand that Rogers's experience in the war has caused him to question the values and habits of a lifetime and to look at the cause-and-effect relationships between wealth and poverty, gain and loss, and power and powerlessness. Frazier tries to convince Rogers and the others that the Walden Two community is an attempt to rectify within its boundaries the inequalities of the outside world. In fact, at least two of the prejudices of the society at large have carried over into the Walden Two community.

First, although Frazier mentions in Chapter 5 that there was a deliberate attempt to "get a representative sample — a true cross section. We failed in some respects. . . ," he does not explain what he means by a representative sample. Does that mean representative from the standpoint of race, sex, background, interests? Nor are we told in what respects this attempt fails. The book gives the impression that all the members of the Walden Two community are white, and all of Frazier's comments to the contrary, that men and women are still sexually stereotyped. While it may be argued that in an ideal situation no mention of race or gender would be necessary or meaningful, Frazier has put himself in the position of pointing out those ways in which Walden Two differs from and improves on the society at large. He, therefore, has the responsibility to inform us of the steps taken by the Walden Two community to correct racist and sexist notions of the larger culture. If any of the characters introduced in Walden Two are anything other than white, we are not informed of it. Further, Chapter 5 is largely concerned with a discussion of the personal attractiveness of the women of the community, though this is never a criterion for evaluating the men of the community. In addition, although Burris notes that the men dress less formally than the women, we have only Frazier's word that it is not a sex difference. In fact, if sexism has been eliminated in Walden Two, then we would assume that women would no longer have to "dress up the goods" and would, therefore, dress for comfort rather than sexual appeal.

Mrs. Meyerson refers to the skirts and blouses worn by female members, but there is no mention made of the slacks and shorts and other informal attire which would seem to be in keeping with the more leisurely life-style of Walden Two.

Skinner's assumption that males are primary and that females are secondary is also evident in the fact that the central characters in the book are males and that Barbara and Mary are mere appendages of Rogers and Steve. Furthermore, characters such as Mrs. Meyerson are employed in fields that have been traditionally "woman's work." Although we are told that both men and women work in the nursery, there are only women working there when the group tours the facility. Miss Ely, the dentist, seems to have broken through the sexual barrier, but, in fact, may be a tokenistic device on the part of Skinner to make Walden Two appear to be non-sexist.

In conclusion, it is not enough to evaluate the things Skinner does explain; we must also be watchful of the things that he does not.

SKINNER'S LANGUAGE

Although it is difficult to separate the form and the content of *Walden Two*, it may be profitable for the reader to evaluate both in terms of the effect that *Walden Two* has on its readers as propaganda. While many of the ideas in *Walden Two* may be new to the reader, and perhaps antithetical to the reader's own views on life, it is obvious that part of the reason that Burris decides to join Walden Two lies in the fact that he believes Frazier's convincing arguments. (Of course Skinner could make Burris join the community whether or not Frazier's arguments are truly convincing, but *Walden Two*, as a novel, has had considerable success based on the ideas that Skinner presents.) But what makes ideas sound convincing? A look at the language provides us with some clues.

Most of Frazier's convincing arguments make use of the truncated passive and nominalization, which results in a prose style which sounds authoritative, scientific, and abstract. These constructions are used by Skinner to focus attention away from concrete issues, so that we are left with a sense that we know what needs to be done, but rarely are we sure of who will do it and to whom. The language Skinner uses is very complex, but a look at the simpler forms might make the steps he has taken toward abstracted language clearer.

A simple, declarative sentence, for example, consists of an actor, an action, and a receiver of the action (these constituents have also been called subject, verb, and object or agent, verb, and patient) as in: "The dog chased the cat." The passive, in contrast, reverses the position of actor and receiver and inserts "by" and a form of the copula (be), resulting in "The cat was chased by the dog." To truncate the passive, we delete the actor (agent), which gives us "The cat was chased." If we nominalize the verb, we are left with a phrase "The chasing of the cat . . ." which is a nominalized truncated passive.

All of these "linguistic devices" can be used quite legitimately by a writer, but they can also be used by people interested in "burying" or withholding information. It is important for the critical reader and writer to be aware of both.

Turning to the text, we can find sentences altered by Frazier which illustrate that the effect on the reader may be to accept a statement as a fact. Once we have accepted something as a fact, we generally don't question the assumptions it is based on.

In Chapter 29, for example, we find "It's not planning which infringes upon freedom, but planning which uses force." We could rewrite this as "It's not someone planning something which infringes upon somebody's being free, but someone planning something and using force." Of course, this rewrite is awkward, and we are not suggesting that writers abandon passives, nominals, etc., but the careful reader must "decode" such sentences in order to understand the relationships of people and actions and to determine who is responsible for a given action. Once the sentence is rewritten, we can ask "what is being planned, and by whom? And how will it affect me?" Further, we must see this sentence not as a fact, but as Frazier's *opinion*.

Another device Skinner makes use of is the passive adjective:

plannned society (Chapter 29)
well-managed community (Chapter 10)
revealed truths (Chapter 23)

In some instances, the deleted actor (agent) may not be important, but before agreeing to live in a "planned society," the reader might want to know who would be doing the planning and according to whose specifications. Clearly, the language we choose to use to persuade someone of something is every bit as important as the ideas themselves. It is important that we be persuaded by reason and not merely fooled by a linguistic sleight-of-hand.

QUESTIONS FOR REVIEW

1. How does Walden Two as a community conform to your vision of an ideal society? In what ways does it differ?
2. How does advertising affect the "choices" we make as consumers?
3. Does freedom exist at the Walden Two community?
4. How might a utopian society deal more effectively with the racist, sexist, and agist attitudes in our culture?
5. How are Castle's arguments discredited by Frazier? Do you agree with Castle's ideas? Why or why not?
6. Are you aware of "behavioral engineering" in the classroom, in church, or at home?
7. When we train animals according to our specifications, are we limiting their freedom? Have we made them unhappy?
8. If art reflects the values of a culture, what might the art be like in Walden Two?

SELECTED BIBLIOGRAPHY

Donner, Henry W. *Introduction to Utopia.* Freeport, N.Y.: Library Press, 1946.

Milhollan, Frank and Bill E. Forisha. *From Skinner to Rogers: Contrasting Approaches to Education.* Lincoln, Nebr.: Professional Educators Publications, Inc., 1972.

Mumford, Lewis. *The Story of Utopias.* New York: Peter Smith, 1941.

Skinner, B. F. *Beyond Freedom and Dignity.* New York: Knopf, 1971.

_____. *Particulars of My Life.* New York: Knopf, 1976.

_____. *The Technology of Teaching.* New York: Appleton Century Crofts, 1968.

Wann, T. W., ed. *Behaviorism and Phenomenology: Contrasting Bases for Modern Psychology.* Chicago: University of Chicago Press, 1964.

NOTES

NOTES

NOTES